Sacred Threshold

Other Books by Paula D'Arcy

Seeking With All My Heart / Encountering God's Presence Today
(The Crossroad Publishing Company, 2003)

A New Set of Eyes / Discovering the Hidden God
(The Crossroad Publishing Company, 2002)

Red Fire / A Quest for Awakening (Inner Ocean Press, 2001)

Gift of the Red Bird / The Story of a Divine Encounter
(The Crossroad Publishing Company, 1996)

When Your Friend is Grieving / Building a Bridge of Love (Harold
Shaw / Random House, 1990)

*Where the Wind Begins / Stories of Hurting People Who Said Yes
to Life* (Harold Shaw / Random House, 1984)

Song for Sarah / A Mother's Journey Through Grief and Beyond
(Harold Shaw / WaterBrook Press, 1979, 2001)

Sacred Threshold

Crossing the Inner Barrier
to a Deeper Love

for Mary –

Paula D'Arcy

Includes the author's own story of her relationship
with Morrie Schwartz of *Tuesdays with Morrie*,
as well as other stories.

*Across The Threshold is
Every Thing –*

A CROSSROAD BOOK
THE CROSSROAD PUBLISHING COMPANY
NEW YORK

Paula D'Arcy

Dedication
for Roy

The Crossroad Publishing Company
481 Eighth Avenue, New York, NY 10001

Typographic specifications: Body text set in Beaufort Extended
10/16 and display type is Present

Printed in the United States of America

Library of Congress Cataloging-in-Publication data is available.
ISBN: 0-8245-2278-8 (hardcover)

04 05 06 07 08 10 9 8 7 6 5 4 3 2 1

Contents

Waiting for Me

Past the walls
that are built around my heart,
past the place where I can see,
where I can wonder to,
past everything I think
will bring me safety,
past where my skin folds
around my body,
beyond what I have been taught
to believe,
something is waiting for me
to reach my hand
into the darkness
of the mystery
and give itself to me.

— VICKY EDMONDS

Don't Miss
Your Life

IN 1984 I PUBLISHED *WHERE THE WIND BEGINS*, a book that has been out of print for several years. It was a collection of stories about people who encountered life with particular courage, and for many readers this book was a favorite among my titles. Three years ago I tried to edit it for renewed publication, but found that both my life and my theology had moved too far past those early days.

Sacred Threshold, twenty years later, is in some sense written in the spirit of that first collection of stories . . . but these stories are seen through the lens of a continuous narrative whose focus is love, love that exceeds the normal bonds and calls out: Don't miss this. Don't miss your life.

There's infinitely more than the experience of love we already know. Push against your borders. Dare to move through the next threshold to the freedom awaiting you.

The individuals in these stories all affected me deeply, and I am grateful for their generosity in allowing me to recount our shared experiences. Each story is told with the explicit permission of those mentioned, and this willingness is further expression to me of the kind of love toward which this book beckons. In particular, two of the stories came about because of my work as a therapist. The first involves a young boy, now a grown man, whom I met while I was a counselor in training. The second involves a now public figure, Morrie Schwartz, who invited me to share with him a beautiful aspect of his dying.

Particularly in the case of Morrie, even as we moved through the hours we spent together, we were aware that what we experienced might be powerful and helpful to others. "Pass this on when I'm gone," were words Morrie frequently repeated knowing that I felt, as he did, a keen sense of our common humanity, as well as a responsibility to give back to this world by helping others discover all that is possible in their lives. Even so, I never had a sense of urgency. Morrie knew that I *would* pass it on when the moment was right . . . when the right book unfolded, as this one has, dealing with the very nature of love's power that was speaking to us so directly almost ten years ago. On a personal level, the "right" time has demanded that I too stand before a critical threshold, just as Morrie did.

The very nature of my relationship with Morrie, which created the rich experience I tell here, was a well-considered exception to the usual rules, as the story will reveal. Indeed, in the course of my many years as a therapist, Morrie was a single exception. Even so, it is important for me to emphasize that the story being told did not occur within the confines of therapy. Therapeutic hours remain, as they must, inviolate and confidential. I reveal only what Morrie expressly asked me to share: the power of our first meeting (since first meetings often shape everything that will follow) and the poignant series of encounters that occurred when two human beings looked together, intensely, at the mystery of both death and life.

A New
Intention

THE PHONE RANG AND I HESITATED. I was working toward a book deadline, and I had been writing in a steady rhythm for hours. Was this a good time for an interruption? In the second it took to consider that, a building tension in my upper body made itself known. I moved reflexively against the familiar stiff ache in my shoulders, the result of sitting in front of a computer for long hours. In the end my muscles made the decision. I decided to get an ice pack for my shoulders, and on the way to the kitchen I picked up the phone. The caller was Roy Carlisle, both my editor and my friend. But he wasn't calling about my manuscript. He had an intention I couldn't have imagined.

A man my own age, Roy had always lived on the West Coast. I'd been a native of New England, living alternately in Massachusetts and Connecticut. Over a span of two decades, he and I had both raised children while living on separate coasts. We had mutual friends in literary circles, but somehow our paths never crossed during those years. Then in 1979, my friend Sheldon Vanauken, author of *A Severe Mercy*, who happened to be one of Roy's authors at HarperSanFrancisco, told me about his new, young editor, someone named Roy M. Carlisle. When my first book was published later that year, "Van," as Sheldon was known, gave Roy a copy. Van's gesture meant nothing to me at the time, but I did remember the editor's name. Twenty-two years passed. Then in November 2001, Roy was hired as senior editor for The Crossroad Publishing Company, with whom I had just signed a book contract. One of his first assignments for Crossroad was to edit the manuscript on which I was working. When we spoke by phone for the first time, Roy remembered Van's gift, walked to his bookshelf, and stood holding the book in his hand.

A handsome man, with gray hair and a beautiful smile (I asked for a picture, to help me personalize the voice at the other end of the phone), I liked Roy immediately. He was intensely interested in every aspect of creativity and life, and the conversations we shared as we worked together on my manuscript were both long and far reaching. We quickly became friends, each of us sensing that our deepening friendship was both important and lasting.

We'd had many heart-to-heart talks about the nature of relationships. Roy was forever questioning what would result if two people decided to reach, together, toward an uncommon experience of friendship and love. This afternoon that question was no longer theoretical. He took me totally off guard by asking whether I would consider dramatically changing my life by joining him on the West Coast in order to commit our friendship to a greater experience of love. Was I willing to accept the challenge of unsettling our lives in order to grow? Did I want to know where the power of love might take us? I drew a very long, deep breath.

We were both well aware that people do not usually make such dramatic commitments to another person apart from a romantic relationship. Without the force and power of romance to define commitment, what path would this experience take?

Later that evening as I thought about Roy's invitation, I noticed a rhetorical question on the last page of a magazine article. *What would it mean for us to make a fresh start, together?* The writer had effectively summed up the essence of what Roy and I were considering with one line. *What would it mean for this world if we all made a fresh start, and began to approach love in a new way?* I closed my eyes.

What if we no longer assumed that love and passion were synonymous with romance, or even that romance was the most desirable form of love? What if there is a truer love that far exceeds the well-known pattern of "falling in love"?

Was it possible to press past romance to whatever might lie beyond it? And would such a love lead you deeper into the heart of God?

I remembered 1989, when I made a three-day and three-night vision quest, fasting not only from food, but also from companionship, from reading . . . from every usual distraction. Alone in nature, I eventually began feasting on the only thing that was there: the natural world. Nature became my food, and suddenly I was communicating with the environment in a way I would never have thought possible. Now I wondered, similarly, where love would feast if the path of romance wasn't there? Deprived of that usual gratification, would a larger love appear? And was I willing to live side by side with someone in order to know? Would we both be changed? Would we find a power and force other than romance, that was equal to it, or maybe greater? Could two hearts, in friendship and partnership, unleash something more than we had already experienced through our separate journeys?

Roy had a compelling sense that this adventure was important to both our lives. Over the years I had wandered far from the East Coast, and I was now living in the southwest, halfway across the country and miles from where I'd begun. In order to respond to his invitation, there were still two thousand miles to reckon with. *Would you consider moving?* he wanted to know. *Would you agree to come together for the primary purpose of opening our joined lives to the draw of God and the reaches of Love?*

No commitments or responsibilities, either to my work or to others, precluded my making such a choice.

But it was a serious decision, with little to go on. My sense of logic wanted to understand *how* this might evolve. What would we be creating? Which threshold were we facing? I was left with an abundance of questions, and no obvious answers. Not a single one. It became clear that if I were going to participate, I would have to act solely on a directive from within.

And amazingly, there *was* an emerging, hidden part of me that was saying, *GO. Do this.* It was a deep intuition, a sense of rightness. Yet that impression, although strong, seemed precarious without logic to support it.

I brought the dilemma to my friends, many of whom caught the vision, recognizing similar longings in their own hearts. They became a chorus of *Yes, a thousand times, YES. Do it. Push past the boundaries. Explore.* But their yes's on my behalf, and my own yes, had fiercely different consequences. My yes would move me two thousand miles from home. This yes would change my life.

There was also a second chorus. This chorus gave voice to the fear crouching at the edges of my heart. These voices wondered, *Are you crazy? This makes no sense. What are you moving toward? What are you running from?* My considering so bold a choice

pressed against rationality and decorum. I was stir-
ring all of our pots. Why did I need to push the borders of our lives so hard? Even when words were not
actually spoken, a feeling was conveyed: Why was I
making such an unusual decision? Please, just continue to live and love in the recognizable, time-hon-
ored ways. Follow the protocols. Honor the set
patterns. Stay rooted.

*But what if we did reach something new? What if
a new dimension of love waits to be unleashed by a
different kind of commitment and a different kind of
longing?*

Was it possible to untangle love and romance so love
might be experienced in a new way?

I heard everyone out. Every reservation expressed
by the dissenting voices was arguably wise with
respect to the rules with which I'd been raised. Those
rules had taught me to limit my levels of risk. The
rules said only take large steps that are well considered and prudent. I knew that. But something else
was pushing me, wanting to be known. Something
longed for me to taste what lay past reason.

Something longed for me to know the embrace of a truer, greater knowledge. What if this was, in fact, the point? And what if choosing the very path presenting itself to me was the right way to go? Maybe new vistas *required* efforts so alien, and a letting go so dramatic. If the portal were common, wouldn't I have stumbled across it long ago? Maybe moving to a West Coast city, far from the southwestern hills that I loved, was reckless only to the mind, but not to the soul. Maybe this was not craziness, but the way in.

In the end, I ventured out far enough to put my house on the market. It was the house of my dreams. Three sides glass, semi secluded, with unobstructed views of sunrise and sunset. No one's mind or heart would tell them to leave such a haven. Now as I watched the deer roaming in my yard at dusk, tears streamed down my cheeks. Leaving had become viable. Redbirds filled the decks, and I considered that they would continue to arrive long after I had gone. Ever since my vision quest in 1989, redbirds had been my continual assurance of God's presence. But redbirds have no natural habitat in northern California.

That fact contributed to the impression that this would be a true leaving. I scanned the landscape slowly. This was a place I had really come to know. I hadn't just *lived* here. I'd been a part of all that surrounded me.

I'd stood on the road in front of my house more than once and silently watched the sunrise with a magnificent buck just a few feet behind me. I'd pruned and watered a grove of oak trees, supporting their fight to exist amidst the cedar; I'd watched their leaves drop and waited anxiously for them to reappear in season. I'd watched the same flock of songbirds come to the feeder each spring, and I knew the precise tree and branch where the redbird preferred to sit. I knew the angle of sun in late December, and where murky puddles would form in the dirt driveway following a driving rain. I knew the rhythm and sound that mimicked a secret knocking in the chimney as the northern winds blew through, and I knew the day or two of glory when the prickly pear cacti first opened their buds and yellow petals were suddenly in sweet profusion. It wasn't just a matter of hiring a van and moving. It was a matter of knowing all these things, and yet going in a new direction.

On a chilly February afternoon a For Sale sign was pounded into the ground at the entrance to my driveway. It blew over in the first strong wind, and I righted it half-heartedly. I'd just consulted my bird manual one more time. No, there were definitely no redbirds in northern California. *Was* I crazy? Not one comforting feeling arose to guide me. Not one recognized marker appeared as a beacon. It was like walking into ether, trusting that sound would occur. But there was no sound. An unrelenting stillness enveloped me, and the striking absence of everything familiar began to change my inner terrain. My reference points shifted. No longer was I preoccupied with what others thought, or anxious to see the eventual outcome this act might affect. I was only asking whether or not, with what little courage I had, I would allow something else from within to lead me.

In time, and only with wrenching attentiveness to my deepest heart, did the usual need for reason slowly disappear.

And sometimes, for rare moments, a clear new vista would emerge, and I began to imagine that we really might walk on this earth differently, led unerringly by an inner force.

But this force clearly gave no ground either to fear or to any attempts to define it. In fact it did not emerge as either sight *or* resolution, and it was relative to no other knowledge. It emerged only as an unshakeable inner knowing. Everything burst with the fresh awareness that two things are always vying for attention: our old way of knowing and a new knowledge, which wants to replace it. *You have to lose the old way of looking*. That thought was embedding itself inside of me.

As my interior landscape shifted, my unique and beautiful home sat unsold, without a bid. I grew weary of continually keeping the house ready to be shown. I never left, for any reason, without glancing back to see whether things were tidy enough. ("Enough" got progressively lax as time went on.) And there were the many interrupted mornings and afternoons when the realtor called and I'd have to pick up my work and head for the park or a friend's porch. It was adventuresome and novel for a month or two. Then it began to lack any romance whatsoever. I had a foreign student living with me at the time, so there were often two of us needing to vacate the house. The final straw was in May when my daughter, Beth, was visiting. Beth was twenty-seven, and busy with her own moves. Having lived in New York City for a few years, then Austin, Texas, pursuing her love for acting, she was now, ironically, making *her* way to the West Coast. Petite, with striking blue eyes and long blond hair, she had come to my home to pack up clothes that still lingered in my closets. No house showings had been set up on that particular Saturday, so I decided it was a good day to thin my own wardrobe. We both emptied our closets, and there were clothes and packing boxes strewn across the entire house. Then an unexpected call from the realtor. Could she come within the hour to show the house? It is not an hour I would ever care to repeat. And our Herculean effort was in vain. The prospective buyers loved the house, but decided not to purchase.

Months edged along, living testament to the fact that despite my plans, I was going nowhere. It felt like a divine comeuppance. I had wrestled passionately in order to respond to my life in a new way, and now that I'd acquiesced and was ready to make the bold move, I was rewarded with inactivity and silence. Stillness within, stillness without. The absence of any outward sign confirming my choice was an irritant to my ego. Doubt reasserted itself easily, and I watched myself slink back into "thinking as usual." *Maybe this wasn't the right step.*

I called Roy and told him about my misgivings, and we talked late into many nights. He listened with great patience and heart as I talked about how slowly things were progressing, but he never shared my doubts. He was absolutely unwavering, a rock. Over and over he repeated his belief that things would happen when the time was right.

Yet by the seventh month I again questioned whether I had misread my inner guidance. Or worse, created it to legitimate my own desire. Was I too emotionally invested in taking this step? That was humorous—finding myself attached to a particular action through which I hoped to live with less attachment! At least I could laugh at myself. And when I was honest, I admitted that indeed, my heart *had* become attached to the idea of moving. I wanted this experience. Aware of this, I painstakingly moved back to an awareness that this action was not about coming *or* going, wanting or not wanting, but about letting Spirit lead the way. It took a while, but I did finally wrest myself, for the millionth time, away from the heart's bond and from my own desire for control. I found the place within me where I was equally willing to move or to stay. The quiet returned.

Attune your heart to the right thing, a voice whispered from within. *Look past what's occurring on the surface.* Beth had given me a collection of sayings from Maya Angelou, and I stood one of them up on my desk where I could see it every day. *"Hope and Fear cannot occupy the same space at the same time. Invite one to stay."* I made my choice. I invited hope.

When Roy invited me to make a fresh start, together, my willingness to do so did not arise suddenly, even if some friends perceived it that way.

Being able to put my home in Texas up for sale was the harvest. But before the harvest were years of plowing, planting, and long, soaking rains. The stories that follow are the rain. They are the moments that began drawing me toward hope, not fear. They are the reason a strong decision was possible. They are a slice in time, a season in my life when I was first aware of the power of loving beyond the bounds. Sometimes I immediately paid attention; just as often I was distracted and preoccupied, even turning away. But the Love was/is relentless.

This season began when I was enduring a difficult passage in my life. I had just experienced the painful end of a marriage, and all my inner edges were raw. My daughter, Beth, was in her senior year of high school facing decisions that would set a course for her own life. She and I were living temporarily on the second floor of a two-family home, sharing one car, so I often walked the two miles to a small office where I practiced psychotherapy.

In fall my walk was a feast of color. Then the damp chill of New England winter set in, making every step an act of courage. That winter there were seventeen snowstorms over a three-month period. Black ice covered the sidewalks in slippery patches. As I pushed my weary body along treacherous streets, I thought grimly that the roads I walked were a perfect mirror of my inner terrain.

That same winter my father suffered multiple strokes and was in the last months of his life. My relationship with him had always held many challenges, and as he weakened, I knew there was little time left to resolve some final things. Then a man named Morrie Schwartz appeared in my life. I had only known him for two or three months when he learned that he had amyotrophic lateral sclerosis (ALS), a neurological illness that suddenly pointed him, without regard for his dreams, toward the end of his life. Aware of the imminence of death, Morrie surprised and challenged me with a request that, if I agreed, would define a period of eighteen months in both our lives.

At this same time I also began volunteering my hours as a counselor on Sunday afternoons in a near-by women's prison. I hadn't expected the experience to mean so much, but Julia, one of the inmates with whom I met regularly, was beginning to affect me deeply. In the prison, in my hours with Morrie, in the regular visits I began to make with my father, and in the difficult aftermath of a broken marriage, I grew increasingly aware of a purposeful force of healing and love laboring to emerge in all our lives. Something was fighting to be known; something seemingly longed to direct each of us to new meaning and sight. And for a brief period, this healing love moved with particular intention through our joined circum-stances, creating a brilliant crucible in which we would all decide whether or not we were willing to be changed, willing to live in a new way . . . willing to wrestle with the full power of Love.

Listening
to the
Power
Within

THE MOST DRAMATIC, FAR-REACHING DECISIONS often begin in quiet moments. It was a Saturday morning in April 1993, and at 10:00 a.m. I was still lying in bed, a thick green comforter wrapped tightly around me, pulled so high it even covered my head. My eyes looked, unseeing, through the small opening I had created for air. The room was still. There is something that enables a person to rise each morning, ready to face the details of the day ahead, but on this particular morning, the magic of that life force was no longer mine. A single thought presented itself to me: *A vital part of me is slipping beyond my reach. If I don't change my life, I will lose myself altogether.*

In some way I knew that I'd already let things go too far. I was swimming far from shore.

As I struggled to focus my eyes on the small square of sky visible through the bedside window, a stream of sunlight found its way through the windowpane and moved in ribbons across the wicker headboard. *How had I allowed myself to fall into such a small place?*

I watched myself as I lay there and saw a woman who had become a stranger to herself. I had been widowed in 1975 (my husband and daughter Sarah were killed in an accident involving a drunk driver) and remarried in 1987. The decision to marry again had been hopeful, but the experience had not played out easily. There were so many factors. I postponed our engagement once because I had reservations. It felt like the decision was too rushed. I was concerned that my fiancé's discomfort around my friends was a hint of strong differences in our natures. But I let myself be convinced that my reservation was unreasonable and only the product of my own fear.

In truth, there *was* substance to my caution, and discounting my own truth was the first herald of the unhealthy dynamic that would follow. My partner's judgments about things very basic to my sense of well-being, such as the way I related to others, my interests and tastes, my appearance . . . all accelerated as soon as we were married. Every shred of my esteem began to erode, until I was enduring steady, reproachful words without resisting.

> Each time I steadfastly refused to stand up to the criticisms, allowing my spirit to be compromised, I myself contributed to the weight that was crushing me.

In reality, I was living with verbal, emotional, and mental abuse, but I couldn't have named it at the time. My only experience was a rising fear. I hated what was happening, but seemed paralyzed to make a change. Eventually one of my sisters called, pleading with me to recognize what was happening to me. Apparently, in spite of my efforts to keep my situation well hidden, it was obvious to her and other family members with whom she'd spoken that something was wrong. Part of me knew she was right, another part felt too afraid to act. Fear had me in its grip.

Moving ever so slightly beneath the quilt that day, I knew that something was willing me, then and there, to finally fight the weight that pressed on me from all sides. But where did that impulse come from? I didn't know. It was simply there.

Sunlight now spread across the accordion-pleated lampshade, breaking into streaks of yellow and red as it stretched across the shade. I watched the colors and found myself thinking of a long forgotten story. I remembered a fairy tale told by Clarissa Pinkola Estes in *Women Who Run with the Wolves*. With no preamble, the story was there, willing itself to break through the dense fog that encased my mind like a linen sac, its drawstrings pulled tight. I searched my memory for a title to the tale. "Sealskin/Soulskin?" Yes. I lay in bed and told myself the story.

There was once a woman who wore the skin of a seal. She lived happily in the sea, fully alive in its great abundance. One night, in order to dance with other seal/women atop a great rock in the sea, she slipped off her skin and laid it on the rock. But when it was time to return to the sea, her skin was not there. It had been stolen. She searched and searched, but it was nowhere to be found. For years afterward she lived on land and wept for the fullness she had once known and for the Great Soul with whom she had lived in the sea.

Then one night as she slept, the woman heard someone calling to her from the ocean, over and over again, until at last something in her awakened. She rose from bed and prepared to leave the confines of her home, having heard the sound of her true self, calling. She walked outside as if in a trance, blindly following the sound, and at the edge of the cliff that dropped to the sea, she saw the "skin" she'd lost. Joyously putting it on, she moved toward the roaring waters. The deeper she dove into the water, the more her life force returned, until finally her lost sight was restored. She was no longer separate from herself. Her skin had been found.

Emboldened by the tale, I got out of bed and pulled on the jeans I'd left in a heap on the floor the evening before. Finally naming my experience had brought something to life. Something within me knew the importance of the tale's wisdom, and knew what I had to do. It had been too long since I'd listened to the truth deep within.

I went to the phone and called my mother, who lived an hour away. She was occupied nursing my aging father, his life radically changed by the effects of surgeries for bladder cancer and several strokes. None of her hours were idle, yet I knew there would be health care aides to relieve her. I asked her to meet me in the driveway and let me take her to lunch. I didn't want to go inside and have to wrestle with my conflicting feelings about my father. Not on this day.

My mother stood waiting for me in the driveway, leaning against the garage door. The years had begun to shrink her frame, and she stood hunched slightly at the neck. She was oblivious to appearance these days, too exhausted by the hours of caring for my father. Her soft gray curls were tucked beneath the cotton kerchief she'd knotted beneath her chin in order to protect her ears against the wind, her upper body lost within the folds of a cream-colored car coat. I noticed that one sleeve of her standard navy blue sweater was pulled down past the edge of the coat's right cuff. She wore stockings, as she always did, in any season, and on her feet were the sensible brown laced shoes that gave her arthritis some small relief.

When my car came in sight, she waved to me with a smile and began moving toward the car. I knew that in just an hour she'd walk slowly back inside that house and again pick up the burden of her chores. It was a twenty-four hour demand that she now shouldered. A demand weighted by the accumulated efforts of fifty years of marriage, during which she had often overlooked her own needs. For this hour, at least, she had a respite from her usual routine.

We found a small, local sandwich shop, and as soon as we placed our order I leaned across the table and told my mother that I was leaving my marriage. That's the knowing I'd faced when I'd gotten out of bed two hours earlier. After three years of hard struggle, I was finally admitting to myself that this was what I had to do. I would have advised any other woman to do the same. But living with the effects of someone's rage had significantly weakened my own sense of power. Now everything in me demanded that I move my daughter Beth and myself away.

The decision had risen up from some deep well of knowledge that was trying to guide me, and I could not continue to ignore that inner voice. I had ignored it for too long, and as a result, I was slowly dying.

Like the seal/woman, I had lost my skin. I had stopped being true to my deepest self.

I told my mother that I was frightened and didn't know how I'd find enough courage to go on. I'd always been the person on whom others had leaned. Even when I had suffered the crushing loss of my first husband and daughter in my twenties, I tried to help others bear the loss. I raised my surviving daughter by myself for ten years, figuring out how to rebuild my life. When I remarried, Beth was eleven, and it appeared to be the end of heartache and the opening of a bright new chapter. But the dream I was reaching for and the reality I found were very different. I'd made a decision that wasn't right for either of us, and lying to myself about it had taken its toll. No amount of wishing, no effort, had made it right.

My mother timidly asked for a few details. For the last five years I had been careful not to speak of my situation. Even though my mother's intuition had told her that I wasn't happy, she still hadn't guessed the realities of our situation. I hadn't been able to afford to have her or anyone guess what was happening until I could face it myself. Now as I described my circumstances, my mother reached for my hand. "I understand," she said quietly.

Then from somewhere deep within, my mother began to speak. Through all the years, we'd never had such a conversation. The force of her words was palpable. She told me that there was within me all the strength I needed. I couldn't have imagined it at the time, but in that moment she was passing on a wisdom that has been passed on, woman to woman, through all the ages. She was directing me to seek guidance from within. She looked at me. "You were always so strong," she said. "I never saw your vulnerability." She was thoughtful for a moment, almost speaking to herself. "But if you are vulnerable, like me, then perhaps *I* too have strength like yours." Her words reached into me. Then she shifted back to the conversation at hand. "Listen," she said. "You can do this, and you must."

She told me that she wished I had someone wiser with whom to speak. Since I had known the beloved minister, Norman Vincent Peale, for several years, and had worked for his Center in New York, she asked what I thought he would advise if I could be sitting with him instead. I smiled. It was so like my mother to assume that someone else would have something wiser to say. But I knew his advice would be no different than her own. I told her that he would tell me to look within for strength, just as she had.

"Then you *are* hearing him say it," she said. She squeezed my hand. "You have to find yourself and act." And with those words, my mother pushed my sealskin across the table of a crowded restaurant and pleaded with me to put it on. She summoned everything she is or ever wanted to be, to be present to me in that moment, and she was momentarily radiant. Feeling as if she had very little to offer, she was telling me exactly what I needed to know: *I was too far from home. Even for the noblest reasons, I had stopped listening to my own soul.*

As she spoke, I realized that she was encouraging me to claim an awareness that was not common to many women of her age. Having played out her own life so differently, within the confines of strict rules and roles, she nevertheless reached forward in one magnificent gesture and helped give birth to freedom in me. I drove home in tears. In willing labor, my mother had twice given me the elements for life.

> That day, I saw my mother in a very different light. She made it clear to me that my life would stay the same until I became unafraid to look within for answers, and then to trust the authority of that knowledge.

That night I started listing the "lies" I needed to unmask. As I wrote, I considered that many things I'd been told and had accepted did not, in fact, ring true.

LIE: A problem is a catastrophe. "Something's wrong" when difficulties arise.

INNER KNOWLEDGE: A problem is a summons. A problem is a call to re-examine your life, looking well beneath the surface. A problem is uniquely capable of revealing what needs to change. A problem is the stumbling stone on which healing may begin.

LIE: Bitterness just happens. Some people are bitter "by nature."

INNER KNOWLEDGE: Bitterness is a choice. We shape our lives by what we pay attention to. Whether or not I'm happy is up to me.

LIE: You can attain certainty and control.

INNER KNOWLEDGE: You can only attain the illusion of certainty and control. They aren't real. We live with mystery, which demands trust and great fidelity to deeper truths, not to external realities.

LIE: Be productive and your life will have purpose. Find romance and your life will have meaning.

INNER KNOWLEDGE: Purpose and meaning come from God. Demanding them from any other place will become a false pursuit.

LIE: You must obey all the "rules." You must stay within bounds.

INNER KNOWLEDGE: Beyond the rules is another realm, waiting to be known. Beyond the bounds of earthly love is where a greater love begins in earnest.

LIE: Life comes at you, and all you can do is dodge the bullets and try to find a way through.

INNER KNOWLEDGE: You can pull life toward you. You can create. There is within me that which is greater than my circumstances.

Telling the truth to myself was an important place to begin. I got into therapy and began to pay attention to the nuances. I hadn't betrayed myself in large gasps. I lost sight of my inner wisdom by taking too many shallow breaths. Now I was learning to take breaths that were deep.

I left my marriage, grieving for both my husband and myself, and Beth and I moved onto the top floor of a two-family home. I sold several pieces of furniture in order to move out on my own. We were missing some vital tables and chairs, but lawn furniture worked well. It seemed to suit this life in transition. Every step required great effort. I strained my wrist tightening the shelves of a six-foot bookcase that I'd put together on my own, fiercely proud of my accomplishment. Then the bookcase collapsed within an hour of my standing it upright. Some of the books hadn't even left the boxes. With tears, I stacked the shelves and the books on the floor and pressed on. I did all of this while still working full time, immersed in other people's lives. It actually helped. It reminded me that we walk together, all of us. I sat in my little office and listened with great compassion to those for whom life presently made little sense.

Never had I been more aware of the heroism it sometimes takes just to get up and find your way through a single day.

As fall became winter, a biting cold set in. And then the snow. I imagine Siberian winters to be no different. For weeks there was no sunlight. I skidded on ice three times, trying to back into my small garage, losing a side mirror each time. The General Motors dealership knew me on a first name basis. Eventually I gave in to nature and parked the car in the driveway, resigning myself to clearing snow from my car and my path every morning.

I was also desperately trying to clear my own heart and mind. A decade earlier I'd learned the hard lesson of setting priorities. I not only *believed* in the necessity of creating a life well balanced between work and play, soul and body, I taught it to other women. I talked about heeding guidance from within. My words were even in print. I grimaced inside: *now* look at me. Fine example *I* was. If I were an alcoholic, I would be saying I'd had a relapse. Why was this so hard? I walked the snowy streets of Boston aware that healing hadn't ended ten years ago. It had only begun. I'd shaped up the outline of my life, but there was much more to realize and important changes still to make. Healing has so many layers, and old habits are relentless. The force of one's culture is relentless. But all of that was excuse. I followed the advice I often gave others and got to work.

However well I understood that the roles I play are not who I am—that I am the Self experiencing those roles—this was still, apparently, something I needed to learn at deepening levels. Because if I had been fully aligned with that Self and her knowledge, I would have chosen differently. It was a sobering realization. But instead of turning the awareness into a self-rebuke, I decided to use it to ignite greater learning.

I began with questions. *Which activities in my life were taking up more time than they were worth? Which relationships nourished me? Which ones didn't? Where should I invest more of my time? How much time did I still spend trying to please everyone? How often was I silent, listening?*

I knew I had choices about whether or not to live in the world differently. But would I actually change? Change didn't require a degree in theology. All the concepts in the world wouldn't benefit me. I needed the discipline required to make the inner journey as primary as I said it was.

I turned a new page in my journal. I wrote, *God is not an idea.* I let those words confront me. *God is a*

reality. A real Power. And I exist because of that Power,
but I have to be willing to know it. Just a belief in God
would not take me far enough. I wanted to live
increasingly aware of the hidden force of God.

Then it became clear: The access point I sought was
the present moment. If I were always living in my mind,
always rushing, always doing, then I would consistently
miss the subtle movement of Spirit.

I needed the spaces in between my actions to
enlarge. I needed pauses. My ear had to be bent to a
different ground.

I created a small checklist: *Guaranteed Ways to
Miss the Hidden God.* My subtitle was: *How to Make
Mistakes and Miss the Voice Within.*

1. LIVE your life at high speed. No exceptions. Run
hard.

2. STAY scattered and distracted. The more clut-
ter and activity, the better.

3. TAKE everything personally. Never evaluate.
Agree.

4. USE blame liberally. It's so invigorating. I wasn't
responsible, *you* were. Everything's your fault.

5. DON'T laugh, especially at yourself.

6. STAY tied to your past. Elevate it to greatness. Live remembering and longing. Or missing. Why do it halfway? Go for it.

7. USE the word "because." "I can't change, because." Because is so little appreciated as a solvent for responsibility. Try using because. This *will* work.

8. NEVER question or think for yourself. Just keep moving and accepting. (Refer to #1 and #3.)

9. CONTINUE to think of God as invisible and distant. Surely not present in this room. At this moment. Not while I'm reading a book.

10. REINFORCE the belief that your life is going to happen soon. This is *not* it, not yet. But one day. Maybe when I finish reading.

My therapist tried to help me acknowledge the part of me that had always known this marriage was not right for either my husband or myself; *I just didn't listen*. I overrode my own knowledge and intuition, paying more attention to outer voices than the one within. Something was trying to guide me, yet I looked the other way. I didn't take the time to let my reservations speak. I trudged through many feet of snow, contemplating that fact.

> Knowing that an inner source of guidance was there (and vital to my well-being) was one thing, heeding it was another.

The point wasn't to draw my own conclusions and then make thoughtful corrections and adjustments along the way. Listening meant taking a different road at the very beginning. Listening meant changing how I related to everything because it meant changing where I responded *from*. What was driving me? Head? Heart? Soul? Which voice had my greatest attention?

Light dawned slowly. Happiness is never found by appeasing others, nor by trying to keep peace at any cost. People and circumstances are movable. I'd been trying to keep the tide from flowing. *Knowing who you are is what brings happiness*. And gradually, I found my way back home. My outside world continued to buckle, but the peace of reclaiming my skin made everything bearable. I realized that I owed sincere gratitude to this season of heartache. It was difficult to learn at such cost, but without this healing, no future relationship of depth and love would ever have been possible for me, nor any sense of freedom.

You can't be free while still hunting either for yourself, or for love. You're free when you know that you already possess everything you need. Relationships are "in addition to" your own worth and loveableness, not the source of them.

I prayed that this tumultuous time would be the cause of equal growth for my former mate. It seemed to me that some persons come together in order to experience harmony and pleasure; others, apparently, join in order to create opportunities for great learning and growth in each other's lives. I had entered our marriage with so little understanding. I left knowing the importance of heeding inner guidance and claiming your own voice. I also learned that in order to truly love someone else, you first have to be in possession of your own skin.

Since I'd walked toward the marriage openly, I now wanted to exit with as much grace. It hadn't gone the way we'd planned. It didn't match our expectations. It involved pain, hurt, and struggle. But it had still been a gift. How else do you describe a crucible in which you are rescued from false gods, and shown so much about the true nature of love? Ethel Person, the celebrated psychoanalyst, says it well, "Something does not have to end well for it to have been one of the most valuable experiences of a lifetime."

After our first year in the upstairs apartment, the new owners decided to live in our space, and asked us to vacate. Beth was almost ready to leave for college, the worst time to make one more transition. A friend stepped into the gap, and we moved into her small rental condominium in Cambridge, which had miraculously become available at just that moment. I gave Beth the single bedroom, and I slept on the couch, knowing that Beth would soon be in a dorm room with even less space.

Then the frustrations began. Whenever I used the stove, the fire alarm was set off by the steam. We lived stepping over boxes. Beth's emotions were on red alert as she prepared to leave home for the first time. It was undoubtedly what Dickens meant when he said, "It was the worst of times." Sometimes at night I would circle for thirty or forty minutes trying to find a place to park on the crowded streets of a busy city. One night I thought I'd have to drive back to my office and sleep there, but a space finally opened. I learned to parallel park with amazing precision, necessity being the mother of at least some dormant skills. Still, I was grateful for this port in the storm.

And even as the outward struggle raged, healing continued. Inner awareness pressed from within. Questions repeated themselves without ceasing: *What did I really want? How seriously did I mean the things I said about letting Spirit lead the way? I felt like a convict confronted with her prior record. I had a history of abandoning myself. I had done it repeatedly. It would take courage to finally change.*

Discerning whether or not someone else was trustworthy had only been part of my struggle. The greater issue was whether or not I could trust *me*. If I could, then other answers would be clear because I would *know* when I was walking into harm's way. I would know because I *did* know. *I knew because a guiding spirit warned me. But I had to be heeding her. I had to be heeding her most of all.*

I thought of the many places I'd gone for advice and all the mentors I'd consulted. The books I'd read. *A*

Grieving Time. Getting the Love You Want. We. Grace and Grit. Journey of the Heart. Every word contributed to my healing, and some of the mentors were invaluable in helping me recognize blind spots and find new perspectives. But all along, *I already knew.*

The force of that awareness overwhelmed me. All the wisdom I needed to navigate my course had always been there.

You Only
Bring
Yourself

I WAS THEIR SECOND CHOICE. The chaplain of a nearby women's prison had called to see whether I would provide an evening program for inmates, but she had no idea who I was. She'd wanted my friend, the well-loved author Macrina Wiederkehr, to come and address the women. But Macrina's schedule was full, and she lived over a thousand miles away in Arkansas. She told them I was local and suggested they call me instead.

I went because the prison chaplain begged me, and it seemed heartless to say no to a Sister. One night. I could at least give an hour for a good cause.

In the parking lot, as instructed, I popped the trunk of my car and removed every piece of jewelry, including my watch. I threw in my pocketbook. I removed my car key from a key ring bursting with keys, each one representing entry into the busyness of my life. From my wallet I retrieved my license. It was a strange exercise with a great deal of power.

> The message was driven home: when you walk through those doors, you only bring yourself.

Your education and degrees no longer serve you. No one cares. Your level of income is irrelevant. Your pretenses are dangerous. Nothing will get through the metal detectors but who you really are.

Sister met me at the first guard station and escorted me. After passing through several metal doors and the first, twisting courtyard, I had already lost any sense of how to retrace my steps. I was now inside the system.

The meeting room was large, and my eyes took in a single microphone standing in the center of a worn, wooden stage. I tried not to show how scared I felt.

At Sister's suggestion I stood by the doorway in order to greet each inmate as they entered. I waited there while she fussed with the microphone and the arrangement of chairs. Finally a bell sounded, and waves of denim began to move down the corridor. I heard them before I saw them, and I stood there comforting myself with the knowledge that no one was forced to show up for this talk. My audience hadn't been coerced into attending. But I also knew that any special gathering was probably preferable to an hour of work duty or sitting alone in your cell. The fact that they were coming did not mean they really wanted to be there or cared at all about what I had to say. It meant that the alternatives were less appealing. Maybe they were simply starved for a face from the outside.

I was surprised by the friendliness and gratitude I sensed as each woman greeted me. *"Thank you for coming to be with us."* They smiled shyly and shook my hand. Some eyes avoided me, but most looked right into my own. My God, I thought. How does it come to this? No woman plans to end up in prison.

Did any of them have advantages growing up? Good homes? Education? Did they have families, children? Surely they loved and were loved. They longed for things. Were we wildly different, or different at all? I couldn't presume to know anything about their pain . . . or even be sure I had anything to say that would matter to them. But one intuition was strong. *If I wasn't going to be real with them, I ought to have stayed home.*

Eighty women filed slowly into the room. Many of their faces were weathered, worn. Their smiles revealed cracked, discolored teeth. Or no teeth at all. Some wore faded headbands that had lost all elasticity. A few women sat alone, but most found seats next to their friends. Once they were seated, the initial spark I'd seen as they welcomed me seemed to fade. Some women now looked sleepy eyed and distant, most simply lost in pain. Only their bodies appeared to fill the space in front of me; their attention might be hard to win.

I was introduced, and my "credits" never seemed so humiliating. I felt sick and wanted to shrink, praying that Sister would stop speaking about what I had achieved. So what, that I had a master's degree? It didn't prove that I'd learned one thing about life, or that I had ever truly loved anyone. It didn't mean there was any reason for them to respect me. I was listening to the usual litany of my accomplishments with such different ears. Would there be any common ground? We were eighty women sitting in the same room, and that was all, unless my heart could reach theirs.

When I finally stepped to the microphone, all eyes were watching me. I took a deep breath and dove in, doing the only thing that made sense to me. I told them my own story of pain and loss, and what I knew of the hard fight not to be crushed alive by pain.

They listened quietly. For a while I had little sense of what they were thinking, with the exception of one woman with wire-framed glasses and curly blond hair who was sitting in the front row. Her eyes, her body language . . . everything about her was taking in my words. She was petite and lively, exuding an irrepressible energy. My eyes moved back to her face repeatedly, my only identified ally. But when I offered to answer questions and hear their comments, the whole room came alive. That was when I knew they had been listening. They were hungry. Ravenous. And they wanted to talk. The atmosphere in the room shifted, and I forgot that I was in a prison. I even forgot that I was the second choice and hadn't particularly wanted to come.

I was only aware of a circle of women speaking with authenticity and power from their burning hearts.

When the bell rang to send them back to their cells, I didn't want to leave and I didn't want them to go.

Sister led me back through the courtyard and the metal doors, guiding me all the way to the waiting area where I would finally exit. *Please come back*, she pleaded. *Give these women any amount of time that you can. Sit with them one on one.*

I couldn't, of course, no matter how my heart tugged at me to do so. My schedule was already full, and my traveling prohibited such a luxury. I wasn't consistently at home. I was a moving target. But Sister either didn't hear me or didn't care about my thin excuses. *Please.* I flashed back to the last part of the evening, when I was distributing the books donated by two of my publishers. The inmates stood around me in clusters, waiting for autographs. The bright, blond-haired woman was there. *Please.*

Sister kept up a good pace, walking beside me and planning the best day for me to return. She apparently didn't hear "I can't." She behaved as if I were accepting her invitation, not refusing it. She moved past my reasons for not returning as if she were water flowing unimpeded to the sea. *Okay, I finally said.* (What else could I say?) *I'll come back just once. I'll return one more time.* She looked at me. *Okay, maybe twice. But that's all I can do.* She finally let that be, and I pushed through the last door and found myself back outside. It was over. I thought I'd peal out of the driveway, but I couldn't even fit my key into the ignition. I laid the key on the dashboard and sat looking through my open window at the moon the women I'd just met could not see from their cell blocks. Another car pulled out of the lot, and the prison froze like a framed picture in the glow of its headlights. And I bent my head onto the steering wheel and wept.

I went back as often as I could. I went when I was too tired to move, jetlagged, weary in my bones. And each time, they breathed new life into me. I sat with them, one by one, in a room too barren and uncared for almost to bear. Even the one scraggly spider plant was struggling for life in its plastic pot. There was an old desk in the room, scratched and chipped, and two wooden chairs with metal legs that I pulled into the middle of the small space in front of the desk. I didn't know why they came. I could fix nothing, I had no answers. I'd have needed a legitimate magic wand and the power to change their past, let alone their present or the future, to bring much hope. But they came so gratefully. *Thank you. Thank you for remembering us. I never thought you'd really come. Thank you.*

I was given permission to give one of the inmates a journal so she could begin to write poetry. She had short, dark brown hair and eyes like a deer that darted continually around the room. Her body was square and strong, tough. She held the journal in her hands and ran her fingers over the cover as if it were sable or mink instead of cardboard.

A beautiful young woman, soft, not hardened like so many, showed up one day at someone else's appointed time. Long waves of chestnut hair spilled over her shoulders and fell across her face. She was already sobbing when she walked into the room, and it was a while before she managed to tell me that the baby she'd given birth to in prison six weeks earlier had been taken from her forever that morning. The inmate originally scheduled to see me at this time couldn't bear to witness this young mother's pain. She wanted to help, but had nothing to offer until she remembered that she had an appointment with me. And even though she'd been waiting for three weeks to see me, she gave her appointment away. When the young mother stood at the door after our time together, she looked back and asked, *Do you think this is how the mother of Moses felt when she let him be placed in the basket?*

Their stories and the obvious love among them was having an effect on me. As one woman said, "Outside these walls you can believe that your actions are isolated. Inside these walls you live a different truth: All our lives are interconnected." A fury of anger would spread like fire. But so did compassion. They pulled for one another. They saved one another. Julia, the woman with blond hair who sat so eagerly in the front row that first night, told me that for the first few weeks after her arrival in prison, one of the women kept placing candies and other little, unexpected treats for her to find under her pillow. It was an act that, if discovered, would bring reprimand and punishment.

> But the giver also knew that in a system stripped of color and sweetness, the spirit had to be nourished.

Julia reflected on the gesture, eight years later, and said, "a letter, a visit, a smile, a covert spoonful of ice cream are magnified a thousand fold in meaning. Underneath the layers of mental illness, drug damage, and appalling manners is still the hope that a little love will fall upon them."

I was stunned by how the inmates kept hope alive for one another, and how potent a force that "little love" was. They did not live "waiting to be released." They lived knowing that "this is it." This day is life. One spring I lived vicariously through the small garden that Julia and her cellmate had been given permission to plant and were tending. First the zucchini and squash were eaten by aphids. The cucumbers survived the aphids only to be eaten by ants. The tomatoes alone remained. In Julia's words, "For weeks we watched, watered, and weeded. She prayed while I removed stems, but the tomatoes remained green. Then one day—in what seemed to be an overnight metamorphosis —an orange yellow splotch appeared. By nightfall, my cellmate was toting a coveted harvest into our room. Using a plastic knife, she exercised more surgical precision than would ever have been possible with a scalpel. Spreading the mayonnaise on fresh, white bread, she gently placed the juicy slices on top. Our eyes met and held as we simultaneously took our first bite. It was not just the taste of the tomato. It was the harvest . . . the work in the garden . . . the miracle of nature . . . friendship . . . survival . . . life . . . all that in a single, simple bite."

That same year I gave Julia some verses from a poem by the Persian poet, Hafiz.

Light

Will someday split you open

Even if your life is now a cage . . .

Love will surely bust you wide open

Into an unfettered blooming new galaxy . . .

A life-giving radiance will come . . .

O look again within yourself,

For I know you were once the elegant host

To all the marvels in creation . . .

From a sacred crevice in your body

A bow rises each night

And shoots your soul into God . . .

A month later I sat with Julia, whom I had grown to love, and we faced the fact that she was in prison for drunk driving. There we were, our two chairs drawn together, knees touching, huddled in the god-forsaken little room where we always met. A single, dirty pane of glass in the door gave the guards their requisite view of us. The paint on the walls was scraped and discolored; nothing here had been scrubbed or tended with any care. But we were oblivious to our surroundings. We looked into one another's eyes and tried to comprehend the irony of our lives being drawn together at all.

The automobile accident that Julia was involved in resulted in the deaths of a father and child, a loss identical to my own. We talked about the ten seconds that had irrevocably changed both our lives. It made no sense for us to care so deeply about one another. To anyone looking at us from the outside, we would appear to be on opposite sides of a great divide. Then we both began to cry, and neither of us could stop. I threw my white cotton jacket over the arms of our chairs and reached for Julia's hand underneath the cloth, hoping the guards wouldn't notice. I hadn't cried that deeply in years, and only once or twice in front of someone else, ever. But I wasn't crying for me. I was crying for her. We each wept for one another.

Julia described the women in the correctional facility as "broken dolls." It was her first impression of their faces when she arrived. She'd expected those faces to be hard and sadistic. Instead they were "cracked and rumpled, looking with longing for someone to patch them up and hold them a few more times. It is hard to look at these women objectively, once you live with them, hear their stories and share their lives. Despite the crudeness, the essence of humanity in these women is very much alive."

While in prison, Julia completed her bachelor's degree. She also encouraged a number of women to learn to read as well as to earn their GEDs. I eventually learned that many of the women who eagerly accepted the gift of my books on that first night could not read at all. One woman told me that she simply held the book each night. It defied my reason to watch their remarkable battle for hope and meaning. The indignities were endless. Random strip searches. Stripping naked before a guard, every orifice probed. Being allowed fifteen minutes to attend a parent's or child's funeral, having been brought there in waist chains and shackles, regardless of whether or not you posed any threat. Being put into solitary confinement for giving shoes or clothing to a fellow inmate who was cold or suffering. In fact, *knowing* that would be your punishment, and doing it, regardless. "Hearts brought to life by wire and chain," is how Julia described it.

And then the mystery of it all. Some of them were freer than most people I knew. Truly free. Again, Julia's words, written while in prison:

> We're both confined, the sun and I
>
> Restricted to a time and space
>
> She watches planets orbit by
>
> I [watch] humans in their race
>
> She knows I crave a different place
>
> Creamy shores of an empty beach
>
> She marks days with her smiling face
>
> Brings freedom closer, within [my] reach

Julia taught me that "what is really of importance and value in life is what you have when you are standing naked in a barren room."

She went before a parole board several times, and even though her behavior in prison had been exceptional, each time parole was denied. She accepted the defeats and continued to use her time within the walls to live. It had been a difficult feat to face her crime, an act that was responsible for two deaths and caused irrevocable scars in many lives. Through her pain she confronted what she could not change. Then, even within the walls of a prison, she learned to grow and thrive.

The last time I saw Julia within those prison walls I smuggled in a gift. The risk was great, I knew. I sweated profusely going through the metal detectors, trusting that the search of my materials (I was leading a three-day retreat in the prison) would not be as thorough after two days of entrances and exits. I got through the guard station with shaky knees. Then I had to get the gift into her possession.

I would not ordinarily break the rules. Perhaps I was remembering the day I had flown from Texas to Massachusetts to see Julia, and the guards, who knew me, would not let me in because they "couldn't find the paperwork" authorizing my well-planned visit. I had traveled two thousand miles, and I never got inside. Or perhaps it was my small defiance against the horrifying injustices in the system. I don't know. I only know that I had always followed the rules, and then I decided to break them.

The retreat was ending, and guards were positioned around the room, watching. I walked past Julia and whispered to her that at some point before I left I would shake her hand and pass something off to her in that motion. She nodded ever so slightly. I felt as criminal as if I were passing drugs or a colt revolver. What I actually held in the palm of my hand was a small ceramic ornament in the shape of the state of Texas, where I was living at the time. It was a piece of me.

Before I left the room that day, I reached for Julia's hand as planned. We smiled and said good-bye, smoothly transferring the gift from my hand to hers. I watched her slip her hand into her pocket and walk slowly away. She waited until she had returned to her cell to look. She told me afterward that the object itself was irrelevant. It was the risk, and the secret that two hearts shared.

After many denials of parole, Julia eventually moved into a group transitional home. From there she wrote, "*I am a spirit free . . . a being who is an extension of earth, sea, and sky. No matter how difficult this present situation is, I will extract the goodness that this system tries to suffocate. The full moon a few nights ago was almost a butterscotch color. My thoughts soared out when I saw it.*

"*My body may have to go through these motions, but my mind refuses to follow. My spirit absorbs all the fire.*"

Goodness and truth were like a whisper within the walls of the prison, sandwiched as they were between the more strident roars of harsh realities. "*The night is as bright as the day.*" (Psalm 139) The mystery of those words, raised against the power of the keys and locks . . . the brutality of many guards . . . seemed so impotent. Yet looks deceive. *Something else is at work in life.*

When I met with the women, sometimes there were long periods of silence. They watched me, their eyes scanning my face for signs of pity or judgment.

> In the end, my showing up as often as I could probably mattered more than any words.

They confessed to me, asked questions I couldn't answer, told stories that may or may not have been exaggerated. And I wondered at the simple fact that our paths had crossed at all. I sat with them in silent communion, knowing I would never be present in such a way with some of my dearest friends. How could that be so? But when a prisoner walked in to see me, I never knew whether I would see her a next time. As far as I knew, we had sixty minutes. And the minutes became our host, the locked door our wine.

Living
on the
Edge with
Morrie

OPENING THE DOOR TO MY OFFICE, I poked my head slowly around the corner to see if the man who had asked to meet with me was waiting. I had no formal waiting room, just a cane chair set up in the drab, narrow hallway with a few magazines tossed on the floor beside it. I doubted that anyone ever really flipped through a magazine in that hallway. The lighting was too dim. But at least the offering was made.

In contrast, my little office had two large windows and wonderful light. Its cheerfulness and brightness were always a surprise after the hallway. A love seat with denim and white ticking was set against the right-hand wall. In the middle of the room, facing the love seat, was my own comfortable chair, a large, swiveling circle of bamboo that supported two giant, multi colored cushions. Behind my chair, the white drafting table I used for a desk was usually stacked high with client files and insurance forms. Framed prints of both New York City in wintertime and Monet's water lilies added color to the walls. On the wicker, glass-topped table next to my chair was a well-worn appointment book and the ever necessary digital clock, telling me how many minutes remained in a session.

In retrospect, it's amusing that I was so tentative as I peered around the door into the hallway that day. The man waiting for me was definitely there. The moment he heard the door squeak on its hinges he leapt to his feet, brushing past me in a flurry. Not waiting for any invitation or formalities, he marched into the room with the words, "I knew you were a woman, but I didn't think you'd be so young." The clear implication was, *What could* you *possibly know.* Then he majestically sat down in my chair and fixed two bright, blue eyes on my face, his eyebrows arched, a look of *you'll have to prove yourself to me* in his every gesture.

Hindsight is sometimes a glorious thing. At that moment, neither one of us would have guessed that Morrie Schwartz was soon to become known to millions by his first name alone, and known to them for his courage and love. This was well before his fame. Before a life-changing diagnosis. Before the amazing opening that would take place within him. Before the two of us had any idea what lay ahead. Before he gave me permission, should I ever decide to do so, to talk about a particular bond we forged and the boundaries we pushed. It was before everything we were about to experience in the crucible of life and death . . . forgiveness . . . and letting go. He was there, meeting me in the midst of my busy day, because a former client of mine had suggested that we meet. I had offered him this hour in between clients, when I had a few minutes free.

On that first day I was only annoyed. He seemed rude and he was sitting in my chair. I had never asked someone entering my office to change seats. But I asked Morrie. Really, I *told* Morrie. I held out my arm, swinging it toward the love seat. He got the idea, giving me my little victory. It mattered little. He had only just begun.

The initial interview, *his* interview of me, was priceless.

Do you have a license to practice psychotherapy?

"Of course, Morrie. I couldn't practice without one."

Hmmm. Do you have a master's degree?

I'm irritated, but try not to show it. "Yes. Of course." Stated firmly.

He was small and wiry, with a slightly disheveled look about him. Seventy-eight years old. A full head of white hair, a colorful cotton shirt . . . but it was obvious that appearance meant little to him. It was not where he placed value.

He leaned in for the kill.

Do you have a doctorate?

"No, I don't. And it's not required."

Yes, but I do!

I didn't reply. I looked at him. He sat forward on the couch, tossing the decorative pillows aside.

Do you see individuals only, or groups as well?

"I only see individual clients."

Well, I work with groups, and it requires greater skill.

I can't believe he's for real. I don't care if he's the most beloved teacher in Boston. I'm not interested. But he's not done.

Are you published?

He's a sociologist, so I know very well what he means. Am I published in scholarly journals, am I bright? Competitive? Knowledgeable? The truth is, I have just published my third book. So I say that. I say that I am the author of three works of nonfiction. Ah. Another notch in his belt.

He glows.

I have authored and coauthored three times as many texts!

For fifty minutes he holds forth. At the end we have learned every way in which he is superior. I'm barely interjecting comments anymore; I'm merely listening to Morrie's monologue. Then with ten minutes left, he asks his next question abruptly.

So, doctor, what do you think?

The words fly from my lips, unedited. I deliver them in an even tone, but I nevertheless deliver them. "I think, sir, that you are possibly the most arrogant individual I have ever met."

Morrie startles, abruptly pulling back his head in a manner I would come to know very well, a look and gesture expressing both surprise and the fact that rapid thinking is going on. Then he slaps his hand on his knee and says, *I didn't think you'd have the guts to say it. You may have promise!* He is filled with mirth, absolutely delighted with himself. He laughs out loud and presses on. *And what do you think is wrong with me?*

My response is again immediate, bypassing the mind. The words spill out. "I think you need to open your heart."

I don't say it with an attitude. I say it simply and plainly. But to my great surprise, he bursts into tears. In a second, the space between us has shifted dramatically. He is no longer following a carefully crafted script intended to subordinate me. He has moved without warning to something at his core. I draw a deep breath and sit still, letting the moment sink in. I ask myself: What vein has been struck and where will we go from here? Little do I guess that in the months ahead I will ask myself this question over and over again, with increasing consequence.

In the following year and a half, Morrie's life story will become well-known when he grants three interviews to ABC's late night feature, *Nightline,* with host Ted Koppel. (*Nightline* finds Morrie when an Associated Press news article reports on the local talks he is giving about death and dying.) Mitch Albom, a former student of Morrie's now living in the Midwest will see one of the *Nightline* broadcasts. After seeing his old teacher on his television screen, Mitch will impulsively fly to Boston to connect with his beloved mentor one last time. And that first visit will grow into Mitch's deeply moving book, *Tuesdays with Morrie,* which will not only chronicle their deepening relationship, but will also include the wisdom Morrie longed to impart as he courageously faced death.

Through Mitch's story and Morrie's own words, millions will learn later what I am now hearing for the first time: Morrie's mother died when he was a young boy, and the impact of that deep wound has been far reaching. Morrie has also been having neurological tests, medical workups. Something is "off" physically, but no test has yet pronounced the source of his vague symptoms. He has moments of feeling slightly off balance. He has fallen. Felt agitated. Fatigued.

I offer to help Morrie with grief work, if he'd like to try. He's still not sure of me. *Why do I need you to do that? I'm sure I can figure it out alone.*

I shrug. It is, of course, up to him.

I only offer the sentiment that sometimes when climbing a steep mountain, it's good not to walk alone.

He's visibly skeptical.

A month or two pass, and we're still deciding whether or not he trusts me and whether he even wants to do grief work at all. He hadn't agreed to meet me in the first place for that reason. He came because of a growing anxiety about his mysterious physical symptoms, and because his former student, and my former client, encouraged him to do so. She thought we'd enjoy one another.

Then a phone call changed everything. The awaited test results are back, and it's the worst possible news. Morrie's diagnosis is ALS, a debilitating illness of the neurological system. There is no known cure. Most ALS patients live only a year and a half to two years following diagnosis.

Things change rapidly. My office is on the second floor of a building that has no elevator, and it's becoming difficult for Morrie to manage the flight of stairs. How will I see you? he wants to know. Would you come to my home? I can think of no other solution. I agree, hoping his home is within walking distance of my office, since my daughter and I are sharing a car. I am relieved when I learn that he lives only a mile away. It's doable. I will be his therapist, if this is what he wants.

My first visit to Morrie's home, and I'm standing at the door, waiting for him to let me in. He already moves quite slowly in contrast to the day we met. The homes in his neighborhood are nicely cared for, but simple. Newton, Massachusetts, the garden city, boasts many large, stone and brick homes with extensive landscaping—crushed stone walkways with flowering trees and well-trimmed bushes. Outdoor sculptures. Monuments. But Morrie's street and his own yard are comparatively modest. The lawns and trees are well cared for, but not lavish.

Morrie lets me in and directs me through the living room to his library, where we sit enclosed on every side by books. His passion for scholarship is evident in this room. Books fill all the spaces, floor to ceiling, and papers and more books are stacked all over his desk.

The crustiness and challenge of our first encounters is gone. Morrie is only welcoming and appreciative today, seemingly delighted that I'm here and grateful that I was willing to leave my office and come to him.

I take a little while to look around. There is a large, oversized window opposite the reclining chair where Morrie is seated, with another set of windows behind him, so the room is bright. Through the windows, tall New England hardwoods offer an effortless elegance, their leaves a brilliant canopy.

I choose the chair from Morrie's desk and wheel it alongside his recliner. He has something on his mind and is eager to begin. He is about to push the envelope, and he has obviously thought hard about what he will say to me, how he will present his case.

First he covers the most immediate challenge, his diagnosis. It is still too large to take in fully; it will require months of breaking it up into pieces small enough to digest. At the moment it's still too arresting. How does a person experience such great and simultaneous changes in both their inner and outer landscapes and yet maintain equilibrium?

You have to move slowly. But one primary aware-ness is unavoidable: *Life is not forever.* More painful-ly, *this life, my life, is not forever. Everything is temporary. I can no longer delude myself that I have tomorrow and tomorrow and tomorrow. I no longer have the luxury of a future. I have the new reality of this moment.*

Morrie is sobered. There are no more rhetorical questions. There is facing death and all the questions it has raised about life: griefs never mourned, words spoken too infrequently or not at all, feelings with-held, experiences not yet tasted. He is very clear. This is work he wants to do, this inventory of his life. He's more than willing. But there is more. He looks straight into my eyes. "I realize that it will be impor-tant to have a therapist help me with all the chal-lenges ahead. Come once a week and do that with me. But I'm also dying."

I know he is leading up to something, but I can't guess what. Morrie's compact frame leans forward with his words, as if to punctuate their intensity. "I need you to come back a second day each week, not as a therapist, but as a human being. On that day, I need you to respond fully to my questions. I need you to walk through this with me with no therapeutic distance. I need all of you to be here. And I need you to say yes to this request."

> In time, Morrie would prove to be skilled at turning my insides upside down.

If only I'd known, this was merely the first of many ways in which he would press hard against the rules, the boundaries. The boundaries governing therapeutic relationships are clear, well —defined, and very important to me. I didn't make exceptions. It wasn't even a debate. "I can't do that, Morrie," I began.

He was ready. "I'm dying," he retorted. "Dying. There isn't time to protect some rule that's crucial in *different* circumstances. We are facing *these* circumstances. And I'm asking you to think larger, to hear one human being's request to another. I'm asking you not to turn away."

I left without giving him an answer, but my wrestling with his request had already begun. *When is the circumstance greater than the rule? When does law concede to Spirit?* I felt angry with him for raising the issue at all. I told him I needed some time to think. He pressed. "Come back a second day *this* week, and tell me." He was incorrigible. He also had no idea that since I usually did not have a car, coming even once a week was a sacrifice. It meant a three-hour block of time from my day to walk to his home, see him, and walk back, thus reducing the hours when I could see other clients and earn my living. Now he was asking for a second day. We said good-bye, with me promising to consider what he'd asked. Frankly, I wanted the whole dilemma to disappear. But as I began walking back to my office, I heard myself repeating the sentiment, *I want all of this to go away.* In that moment I realized that Morrie had to be feeling exactly the same way. But he didn't have the luxury of a choice, like I did.

My thoughts during the next days were troubled. I was busy with work, but Morrie's request intruded whenever work didn't keep me fully occupied. The answer was no. That was clear. No exceptions. I didn't need to get in over my head. I didn't want to. I wanted to have the clarity I was enjoying before a seventy-eight-year-old man started pushing me to think of life in a much larger way.

I promised to call Morrie by Thursday to tell him whether or not I would show up on Friday as a human being. Wednesday night was long. I knew what the answer had to be, but I couldn't find peace in refusing him. Why? What flashed before me was the face of a young boy whom I had counseled while I was still in graduate school. Scott was eleven years old, winsome, defiant, and also particularly skilled at pushing up against me. His parents brought him to the university counseling program because he was experiencing angry outbursts at home, in the classroom, and on the playground. His excellent grades were falling, and no one had been able to figure out what was wrong.

When he and I were first introduced I smiled. He looked like a Norman Rockwell creation. Freckles, long reddish blond bangs that swept his eyes, he was an all-American boy. But *he* wasn't smiling because he didn't want to be counseled by me or anybody. His first sentence to me, spoken with a clenched jaw, was predictive: "I don't want to be here, and I'm never talking to you." So there.

It was a rocky experience for a fledgling therapist. For weeks I sat in a small green room with an uncommunicative client while my advisor and peers watched my misery through a one-way mirror. Hard enough to fail at all, but worse to fail so publicly. Eventually my advisor used my agony as an opportunity to talk about clients who were unwilling to change. His words were direct: No one can be helped who isn't ready or at least willing. In truth, Scott's *parents* were the ones who were willing, and they had brought him to work with me with a hopeful eye toward his healing and changed behavior. But Scott himself was not interested at all. My advisor's recommendation was that the therapy be terminated. I'd wished for an end to my miserable struggle, and here it was. These were the words that would set me free.

But when the words were actually spoken I was face to face, not only with my release, but with something else I hadn't realized: I cared deeply about this boy. Yes, I would certainly do poorly in my practicum because of him, but that was a grade. What would *he* be carrying on into his life? That mattered to me. Apparently, given the level of my upset, it mattered a lot.

I was on my advisor's doorstep three days later, early on a Monday morning.

All my feelings poured out in one stream. *Listen, there may be another way.He hates that room. It's not a room for little boys. Please give me a chance to take him away from the room and be with him in another way.*

My advisor was thoughtful and asked what I had in mind. *Walking with him, that's all. When he comes for his therapy, I'll take him for a walk. We'll kick leaves and visit the animals in the agricultural barn at the edge of campus. We'll climb hills. I'll go with him where a boy needs to go.*

And to the credit of an adventuresome mentor, he said all right and agreed to let me give it a try. That try became so much more than techniques of therapy and text-bound lessons about human behavior and theories of personality.

> **The try exceeded the rules and became a profound experience of the power of love to invade the human heart.**

Scott and I began to walk together, and we kept walking through three seasons. We always went outside, even in the cold and rain. For the first few weeks there were few, if any, words between us. We merely walked together side by side. When we finally began to speak, it was about trees and rocks and snakes and birds. Boy talk. We ran. We pushed and shoved. We laughed. In the springtime, his mom drove us to the ocean for one of our walks, and that day we collected shells. Earlier, while still meeting inside, we'd made strings of the love beads that symbolized the new consciousness of love sweeping across the country. Now as we walked, we talked about that love . . . about relationships and about how people affect one another.

I was continually responsible to my advisor and my peers to describe the progress of this unusual relationship, but I never knew what to say. It fell within no category of therapy that I was studying, but clearly it was working. Scott's parents eventually called my advisor to say that he was doing better in school, and his anger was slowly dissolving; he no longer disrupted the classroom, and he was once again full of life. I could not fathom *why* these good changes had come about, but I was grateful. When we finally terminated, the good-bye was emotional for both of us. We had truly encountered one another, he and I. It had not been superficial. We'd let it become real.

Following my graduate school years, I began working as a counselor at a small community college. While there, I met and married one of the English professors, Roy D'Arcy, and together we imagined our future. I became pregnant almost immediately, and the birth of our daughter, Sarah, assured us that our dreams were coming true. We had no money, an old house that needed lots of work, and a surplus of love. I don't remember anxiety or cross words or even tension. It was easy. We were sailing without trying.

Eighteen months after Sarah's birth I was pregnant again. Thrilled with the news that we were expecting another child, we took a fateful three-hour trip by car from Connecticut to Massachusetts to share the joy with my parents.

On the return trip, twenty miles from home, a drunk driver rearranged my future.

Eleven days later I sat before an open grave while Sarah and Roy were lowered into the earth. Then I went back to my parent's home, three months pregnant and shattered in heart and spirit, to see if I could find my way.

Initially there were many visitors, but I was too enveloped by pain to make much effort. Most of the words meant to encourage or support me only made me feel worse. My life fluctuated between anger and heartache. The anger, of course, was only a thin veneer. At best it offered small moments of respite from the wrenching pain. Everything inside of me hurt. Still, it was preferable to experience anger than to swim continuously in the grief.

One particular Sunday afternoon when I was still recovering at my parent's home, my mother came to my room and told me I had visitors. I greeted that news with a harsh remark, the full force of growing despair expressing itself. My mother rightly left me to my own hardness, telling me to greet my guests or not. She slammed the door behind her.

The slamming of the door got my attention, and I briefly saw myself and the misery I was inflicting all around me. I hated who I was becoming. Chastened, I pulled on a clean shirt and walked into the living room, hoping to listen to the voices in the kitchen until I figured out who was there. To my surprise, there was a man standing alone in my parent's living room, looking out the window toward the bay. He turned when I entered the room, and I stared in disbelief. Neither the intervening years nor his maturation could prevent me from recognizing that face. Same freckles. Same reddish blond bangs, now swept to the side and slightly gelled. Now, clean shaven. But I knew him. I knew him well. Scott.

As I was trying to believe what I was seeing and make sense of Scott's presence, he was already across the room, his full-grown hands extended to mine. "Yesterday I heard about your accident," he explained. "I was at the university and ran into your old advisor. He told me." No response found its way past my level of shock. I couldn't answer him, couldn't form any words. *Oh, my God.* That single thought filled me and kept repeating itself. Here I was, angry, unreachable. And perhaps the one person against whom my heart had no defense had just walked through the door.

He quietly reached out and took my hands in his. "My parents are in the kitchen," he explained. "I begged them to drive down here with me, to help me find you." I watched him, but I still couldn't speak. He went on, "Paula, at the hardest time of my life, you were there for me." His voice dropped to a whisper. "So I wanted to be here for you." He had come to pass back the love.

Scott guided me to the couch where we sat in silence as he continued to hold my hands. His arrival, his walking across that room to hold my broken heart . . . who could measure the meaning of such a gift or the extent of healing it carried? The sheer directness of the love.

And now I realized that Morrie's request was for a similar love. Morrie was saying, please, exceed the boundaries . . . make an exception to the rules. I felt like a lawyer who'd been searching for the compelling legal precedent. Now I'd found it. Step over the threshold, Morrie was saying. Suddenly it was so simple and so clear: I had *walked* with Scott. We walked together. That's what our experience had been. Now Morrie was asking me to walk with *him*, as well, but to walk with him toward death. He was asking me to put aside the rules of convention and play by the inner rules of love.

I called on Thursday morning to say I would be there on Friday, not as a therapist, but as a human being. The phone call took two minutes. What would follow might not be as simple, but there was no longer any question that I would go.

When I arrived on Friday afternoon, Morrie deliber-
ately led me to a small den tucked behind the living
area. He was wise. If we were changing the game plan,
we should also change the room. Other than Morrie's
study, each of the rooms in his home were open and
uncluttered, making the few pieces of art and the
scattered paintings very distinct. I settled into a small
chair opposite Morrie and waited. I didn't need to
worry about how this would go. Morrie was in charge.

First question: "Were you raised as a Christian?" I
was taken aback, but I probably shouldn't have been.
It was a continuation of his initial interview a few
weeks ago. But this time the subject matter was my
life, not my career.

"Yes," I said carefully, "I was raised in that tradition."

"I was afraid of that," he shot back. "So here are
the ground rules: never, ever speak of it. I don't want
to hear about Jesus. There was too much anti-
Semitism in my upbringing in New York.
Understand? The scars are still painful."

I understood. I wasn't intending to initiate conversations anyway. I was only intending to respond, and
I said that.

Morrie rushed on. "I'd like to read your *three*
books." The inflection made me laugh because the

effect was clear: your *three little books, in contrast to my ten or twelve*. That was fine, I'd be glad to bring the books to him, but I questioned out loud whether or not the books might lead to areas he'd just announced he didn't want to hear about. He was unperturbed. "Any book can be closed," he retorted.

He asked some questions about my family of origin, my place in the birth order, and my relationship with my dad, since he, a father, was now thinking about his own relationships with his sons. I kept wondering whether I was passing muster. But I answered everything honestly and fully, even though our format still felt awkward. On Tuesday I had agreed to be his therapist; three days later we were two souls discussing the experience of life. Yet Morrie bridged it gracefully because he wasn't concerned about whether or not I was comfortable. In his eyes, I'd come through the barrier when I agreed to be there for him. He was only intent on the journey ahead. After that meeting I dropped off my three small books, which he received with a smile.

The books were sitting on the table in front of him when I arrived the following Friday. I saw his first tenderness that day. Holding the copy of *Song for Sarah* in his hands (*Song for Sarah* is the story of the deaths of my husband and first daughter, Sarah), he said, "So this is why you are a good guide through grief." There were tears in his eyes. "I'm sorry," he said. "It must have been hard. You loved her." He looked at me. "You said good-bye after she'd already gone. I have to say good-bye knowing that I'm going."

I was painfully aware of that. And to me it seemed immeasurably more difficult to face saying good-bye in that way.

Even though I'd spoken of my loss on stages and in seminars all over the world, sitting with someone face to face who was learning about my history for the first time had a very different character.

Morrie's simple *I'm sorry* touched me, and that day set a tone for the many Fridays to come. Now it was clear. We were going to go all the way into both our lives. No holding back. No niceties.

As he kept reminding me, he was dying; there wasn't time to waste.

The playing field was treacherous, yet it also offered the great gift of knowing that our moments were numbered. That's always true, of course. But since the mind refuses to know it, we seldom live from that power.

Over a period of time these Friday conversations became a fabric in both our lives. Morrie was fascinated by my weekend travels to lead retreats. Who was there? Why were such deep connections made during those hours? He had me talk about everyone I had met, and he drank in the stories. He ventured, "I wish you had the same look in your eye when you spoke about me. What connects you so quickly to total strangers?"

I laughed. "That about which I am forbidden to speak!"

"I see," he said, but without the familiar frost to his words.

After having been in Alabama one particular weekend, Morrie said that I was unusually full of life . . . that my eyes had a different brightness. He demanded the story from the weekend, but I hesitated, finally confessing that telling the story would move closer to an area that felt uncertain to me. I didn't want to offend him or disregard his wishes. I didn't know how he regarded what I considered to be the appearance of Spirit in our ordinary affairs. Maybe he thought it was pure nonsense. He waved off my sentences with the back of his hand, impatient with me. "Tell the story!" he insisted.

My friend Marcia organized the retreat. She is an amazing woman, I told Morrie, with a strong, deep heart and faith. Things that tip the scale toward the miraculous will frequently happen when I'm with Marcia. On Saturday afternoon I'd finished speaking and was standing just inside a church pew, autographing copies of my books. As I reached out for the next book being held out to me, I saw a hand extended through the crowd of people pressing toward me. In that hand was a small object that someone obviously wanted me to take. I couldn't see the person, only the hand. I took the offered gift and dropped it into my purse, quickly forgetting that I'd done so. I continued to greet people and sign books until I went on to a special dinner. By the time I reached my hotel the hour was late. I was tired, but I still spent some time preparing the talks I would give during two identical church services the next morning.

The next day I ordered my breakfast from room service and ate yogurt and fruit while going over my notes. I absentmindedly sipped tea. It felt as if I should add something else to my remarks . . . but what? Only then did I remember that I had dropped something into my purse the day before, and I opened my pocketbook to find it. Stuck to the side pocket was a small square of cardboard. I pulled it out and examined it. Pinned on the cardboard were two tiny bronze baby shoes. Underneath the shoes was a scripture reference, Acts 1:8. I had no idea what that verse was, so I found the hotel Bible and looked it up:

> But when the Holy Spirit comes upon you, you will be given power, and you will be my witnesses in Jerusalem and all Judaea and Samaria and as far as the end of the earth.

I studied the words, then the shoes. And in the next moment, quite unexpectedly, I saw the face of a particular man who'd been in attendance at the retreat all weekend. I was certain, without knowing why, that it was important to give one of the shoes I was holding to him.

I tried to dismiss the thought because it was so silly. The person I was picturing was a large man; what would he do with a tiny shoe? And how would he regard me if I offered it to him?, not to mention how ridiculous it would all seem. I returned to my preparation, but the shoes kept intruding. They seemed to have a life and a will of their own. Apparently nothing else was going to be done until I dealt with them. So I finally resolved to give the shoe to the man if indeed I saw him again that morning.

I arrived just in time for the first service, and I was relieved that the man and his wife were not in attendance. Following the service I counseled with a couple trying to decide whether or not to be married. When I rushed back into the sanctuary it was just before the second, and final, service was ready to begin. I sat down in one of the front pews, but even with my eyes closed it was difficult to screen out the growing activity in the church, especially with latecomers moving in on either side of me. I felt frustrated by the lack of solitude, but it wasn't for any holy reason. My eyes were shut because I was already anticipating my flight back home, trying to figure out how I would ever find the extra twenty-five hundred dollars I badly needed to make a house repair. It was that mundane.

When the organ prelude signaled the start of worship, I opened my eyes and glanced to my right. There sat the very person to whom I had resolved I would give the baby shoe "if I saw him." My stomach knotted. I was really going to be forced to do this. What amazing coincidence, him sitting beside me. But before I could speak, he nodded to his wife, who had moved to the other side of me, and he handed me a small white envelope. I didn't want to lose courage, so I thanked him and said that I had something for him as well. "Open this first," he encouraged. I ripped open the envelope and found a note thanking me for the weekend retreat. It was signed John and Judy Bentley. There was also a folded piece of paper. I pushed back the fold and looked at a check for twenty-five hundred dollars.

I looked first to him, then to his wife, Judy. He spoke first. He said that as he and Judy had prayed that morning, he'd felt led to write me a check. He had no idea whether I was rich or poor, whether I needed the funds or was abundantly wealthy. It didn't matter. His prayer led him to write the check. The first amount he'd written down was two thousand dollars, but something from within corrected him and he changed the amount so it would be twenty-five hundred dollars. That's all he knew. "And you had something for me?" he went on.

But the service was now mercifully beginning. I could hardly give him a miniature baby shoe pinned to a square of cardboard in exchange for that check. The freedom of his gift stunned me. For the next hour it was hard to concentrate, and I was grateful that I'd already given my talk once that morning. As soon as the service ended, I was swept up in greeting people and saying good-bye. Within two hours I'd be flying home. Frankly, I was grateful for the commotion because it allowed me to avoid John and Judy Bentley. Their gift was so great. How would I ever thank them adequately? What could I say?

Marcia and her husband, Audie, had planned to take me to lunch before driving me to the airport. Marcia was keeping track of time, and when she said that we needed to leave, I began gathering my belongings. That's when I heard her ask John and Judy Bentley to join us.

As soon as we'd all been seated in the restaurant, John turned to me. He remembered what I'd hoped he'd forgotten. "Didn't you have something for me?" he asked. There really wasn't much choice. I pulled the baby shoe out of my pocketbook and handed it to this big, strapping man. I stumbled over my words. I told him the story of receiving the two shoes, one of which I was wearing on my lapel. I told him about my strong sense that the second shoe would be meaningful to him in some way. As an afterthought I drew his attention to the scripture reference printed on the card, Acts 1:8.

John listened with emotion, fingering the card in his hands. Acts 1:8, he finally said, was the very verse in Scripture that had turned his life around the year before at a men's retreat. Because of that verse, he was now the kind of man who prayed and listened . . . and wrote checks when the spirit guided him to do so.

The specific meaning of the shoes was still unclear to us. But the importance of the verse was undeniably powerful, to say nothing of John's gift to me of precisely the amount of money I needed. None of us doubted that in time every aspect of this story would make sense. We parted knowing that our lives were irrevocably linked.

> Morrie listened with keen attention and then grew pensive. He asked me how I explained such things. "The Spirit of God," I said.

I had no other explanation. What else encompasses such mystery and coincidence? Or beauty? Morrie nodded his head, still deep in thought. When he led me to the door he was still pondering the story.

As the weeks passed Morrie's strength declined. His legs weakened noticeably, and soon he moved from cane to walker to wheelchair. Even his arm muscles showed signs of being compromised. The question was always there: What would the future hold? At this same time my friend Pat was a live-in companion to a woman named Helen, a vibrant and beautiful woman in her fifties who also had been diagnosed with ALS. With Pat's encouragement I flew to Dallas to meet Helen and learn what might be ahead for Morrie.

The progress of ALS is different for each person. Helen, although close to death, was still able to walk with a shaky gait. ALS affected her upper extremities first. (It was the opposite for Morrie.) But in spite of her labored breathing and the attending difficulty she had with speaking, she lovingly and willingly agreed to meet with me. I found the home where she and Pat were staying, and the three of us went to a nearby park for a picnic. The picnic was liquid only for Helen. She could no longer chew or swallow solid food. She graciously let me feed her, raising a cup of liquid to her lips.

It was sobering for me to witness how ALS progressed, and of course Morrie was anxious to know what I had experienced. He and Helen began to communicate via brief notes, and even though they never met, her death was a blow to him. She knew what I could never know, and her encouragement had been a great boost. She, like Morrie, rose to meet the disease with a stunning spirit. And ironically, in their prime, they had both particularly loved to dance. Above all else, Helen wanted me to be sure to tell Morrie that she'd learned to dance without ever leaving her chair. "Tell him it's possible. Tell him I dance every day." By the end, Morrie had learned that secret himself.

I always arrived on Fridays prepared for any conversation or request. But I was still unprepared the morning Morrie looked up and said, "I want you to pray."

"Out loud?" I asked.

He nodded. I took a deep breath. We were a long way from where we'd begun. He said very little after I prayed, but the intimacy of sharing this experience had affected both of us. Morrie was seldom at a loss for words. His next question was always ready. But not on that day. On that day we looked at the trees outside his window, and we talked about the hibiscus plant near his recliner whose blossom was ready to unfold. The unfolding of those blossoms had become a potent sign of the miracle of life for Morrie. He watched them carefully, once calling me to announce the imminent appearance of a new blossom, and wondering whether I could arrive in time to watch with him.

The next Friday Morrie asked whether I would be willing to join him when his Buddhist meditation teacher came to visit. A Jew by birth, Morrie had maintained a Buddhist practice for years. It shocked him that I immediately said yes. He told me later that he was certain I would decline the invitation.

But the afternoon when his teacher and I were scheduled to meet with Morrie, he was having a choking spell. As time went on, these became more and more common. When it was critical, as it was that day, one of his therapists would arrive to pound on his back until the accumulated mucous had been broken up. Morrie's own chest muscles were too weak for him to do that for himself any longer. While he was being helped, his teacher and I sat in the living room and talked. I was immediately drawn to her, and by the time Morrie was ready to see us, she and I had already established a wonderful rapport, and our two hours with Morrie were delightful. He confessed afterwards that he had fully expected us to have a heated conversation. (Knowing Morrie, he had hoped so.) But there was no divide and no conflict. We all settled on love. Morrie said later that it was amazing to experience a common spring much deeper than the boundaries of our different traditions.

> As Morrie's strong determination to die well began to change him, the change was increasingly visible.

He grew more and more convinced of the importance of each day, and he began asking me questions about my strained relationship with my father. I didn't always want to speak about it, but Morrie had a way of pressing. His own relationship with his sons was so important to him . . . maybe he felt a mission to push until I too experienced that kind of closeness with my father. At any rate, because of our conversations and his repeated inquiries about whether or not I'd taken any steps forward, I began to visit my father on a regular basis.

> Forgiveness and healing became a constant conversation between Morrie and me.

In addition to asking me about developments in my relationship with my father, Morrie repeatedly wanted me to repeat a story I'd told him about the day I met the drunk driver responsible for the deaths of my family. It had been a defining moment for me, even though I didn't meet him until seven years after the accident. At that time, the driver was subpoenaed as a witness in a civil trial concerning existing highway conditions at the time of the accident. I had never seen or met him before, in any of those intervening years. This was our first meeting. But seven years worth of effort to forgive, to even become *willing* to forgive, culminated in a powerful encounter between us that day. The experience was a forceful lesson. It taught me that the power of forgiveness is not only freeing, but it is one of the highest expressions of love.

So Morrie and I talked at length about forgiveness, especially in regards to my healing the wounds in my relationship with my father. And then the unthinkable happened. Morrie took some detail that he'd gleaned from one of our conversations (I'd answered a particular question of his with a great deal of openness and vulnerability), and he used this knowledge to make a smart remark. I was certain that he'd intended it to be funny. But it hurt deeply.

As soon as his words were spoken, I doubled up inside. I continued with our hour together and left without saying a word, but as I walked back to my office, the force of Morrie's comment found its mark.

I'm not sitting in that room an extra day every week so you can use what I tell you against me, I thought. I was sufficiently hurt to seriously considered ending the Friday visits. But my friend Eddie, a consistent prayer partner, encouraged me to go back one more time. He also promised to pray during that hour. I'll always be grateful that I sought and heeded his wise counsel.

My next meeting with Morrie was on our therapy day, but when he met me at the door his face was stricken and he held out his hand and said, "Don't speak. Please, don't say a word." Then he wheeled his chair into our Friday room, and I followed. Once we were inside he wept as hard as I'd ever seen him weep. When he gained some control he could only choke out the words, "I know what I did." I'm aware that printing these words, now, on a piece of paper can't begin to convey their force that day. He said the same words over and over, "I know what I did."

Apparently when I'd left his home on that previous Friday, Morrie immediately knew he had crossed a line . . . he realized it. But it wasn't a mere insight. He described it as moving through a doorway and over a threshold, suddenly aware of the full impact of every word he'd ever spoken. *We wound one another*, he kept saying.

WE COULD LOVE, AND WE CHOOSE NOT TO. His sight became so clear, and the consequence of his action so forceful, that it was almost more than he could bear.

For me, it was perhaps the deepest confession and admission of transgression I had ever witnessed.

He begged my forgiveness and asked for another chance. I agreed. But separate from my own personal involvement, the experience of Morrie's intense awareness had great power. I could only relate what I was feeling to something described in the final chapter of C.S. Lewis's *The Great Divorce*. In the story, a group of occupants from hell take a one-day bus excursion to heaven. Once there, they observe a chessboard set on a silver table. The reader is told that the silver table represents Time. The chess-like figures moving to and fro on the board represent human beings, busy with the affairs of their lives. But standing behind the table, watching, are figures that Lewis describes as "a great Presence." And each Presence is the Soul that the chess-like figure truly is, longing to reach the small figure that is caught up in the game on the board.

That afternoon as I listened to Morrie, it felt as if the great Presence watching *him* had gotten through.

Almost ten years have passed since that morning, and the force of the experience has not diminished. On one level, Morrie's heart had a penetrating awareness of his actions and their consequences. But it was so much more. I watched him be overtaken by a knowledge that permeated his very core, and substantially changed something in his nature. From that moment on, to my eyes, Morrie was different. A commanding compassion had taken over.

A week later, on Friday, master always of surprise, Morrie asked me to tell him anything I understood about the power of Christ. "Not from a book or a Bible," he cautioned. "What do you personally know?" As I talked, Morrie wept. Tears streamed down his cheeks involuntarily, and this response both puzzled and frustrated him. "Why am I crying?" he asked. "I don't even *want* to be moved by what you're saying, and I don't believe it. So why do I cry?"

I didn't know, but I told him what I suspected: that the Spirit hidden deep within us recognizes truths our minds do not consciously know. And in spite of the barriers and limitations *we* impose, in spite of our fears and our refusals, in spite of our determination to limit Spirit to certain names or beliefs . . . there is nevertheless a level of awareness within us that exceeds all names and definitions. And this awareness responds from a knowledge the mind does not possess.

We left it at that, and I walked back to my office in a freshly falling snow, thinking that more than anything else, Morrie and I *were* sharing what it means to be a human being, just as he'd requested. We were exploring meaning. We were asking: What does it mean to be alive? Is this human nature our only nature? Is something else trying to emerge? What will we do with the life we were given? How will we live? What limits are we willing to push? How much are we willing to see?

The specter of death was always there. I was able to move in and out of Morrie's home and momentarily forget his diagnosis, but he stayed there. He was living with an unyielding psychic reality: *He was about to die.* In addition, on the mundane level, it was increasingly difficult for him to find a comfortable physical position. I'd assumed that when muscles atrophy and limbs no longer move, there is no pain. But there was considerable discomfort, and the aides would sometimes work for long periods with blocks of cotton or lamb's wool to help Morrie lessen the shooting pains. He always apologized if I had to wait while they positioned him. His consistent awareness of others, even while immersed in such straits himself, was remarkable.

One afternoon that winter I arrived at Morrie's door blanketed with snow. Snow was falling at about an inch per hour, and in the thirty minutes it took me to walk from my office to Morrie's house, I became covered with white. As I hung up my coat and stood shaking out my hat and mittens, Morrie questioned how I could be so wet with snow after just walking from my car to his doorway. That's when he learned that I didn't have a car; my daughter needed the car for afterschool drama rehearsals, and I walked to see him most of the time. The force of that revelation was strong for Morrie. *You walk here twice a week just because I asked you to? Out of love?* It hadn't seemed like a big deal to me until I watched Morrie's eyes.

> Later he would say that knowing that I walked the two miles to his house probably had greater impact for him than any words we ever spoke.

One Friday Morrie asked me to tell him how I'd turned the corner in my own healing. What was the point at which full acceptance of my changed life began? I shrugged and told him that it had been a process, making it extremely difficult to pinpoint a single "aha." Especially now, years later. He looked at me in his direct, inimitable way and said, "I'm dying. Go home and figure it out and return with an answer."

With such a directive from Morrie, I was impressed to go home and figure it out! I re-read old journals until I thought I'd found the key he was looking for. Acceptance and healing had begun in earnest for me when I became willing to see beauty in exactly what I'd been given. As soon as I stopped holding onto memories, or even to the way I *wanted* my life to unfold, I began taking in how it *was* unfolding. Morrie listened carefully and then asked, "How do you think this translates to my situation?"

I had anticipated his question, and had an idea. Morrie's memories were not only remembrances of cherished times, but also memories of having a fully functioning physical body. I suggested that we honor together, sense by sense, what it meant to experience life within a human frame. We'd talk about the days when he was fully active. I'd help him remember experiences and events. And then we'd grieve the loss of these abilities and experiences until he felt ready to let the memories go with gratitude and love. It was a process that suited Morrie. He would begin to let go, bit by bit. Since ALS had first affected the mobility in his legs and feet, that's where we began. I prompted him with questions to get us started.

What was it like to be a human being and have feet that took you wherever you wanted to go? To dance? To climb mountains? To run? To move from place to place? As Morrie began remembering, tears came easily. He was increasingly aware that being able to walk and move about freely is a great gift. He talked about all the places his feet had taken him, and his memories encompassed both times of pleasure and times of pain. As I listened to him, I looked at my own life. I was borrowing his eyes, which were sharpened by the imminence of death and loss. Morrie told stories and cried and remembered until he was ready to say, "I'm grateful to have known this joy, and I accept the fact that this experience is no longer mine. I let it go with gratitude."

Sense by sense, week after week, Morrie said good-bye to the gift of life.

His hands. *Where had they been? What had they held, touched?* Now he was seeing, clearly and powerfully, the potential within each of us to heal or express love through touch. Then he posed a different question. What had his hands *not* touched? That question generated a strong response, similar to the moment when he'd hurt me with a biting remark. This time, a man who could no longer move his hands at will wondered why he'd missed even one opportunity to reach out when he was able to do so.

Because of these absorbing conversations, I walked around freshly aware of how stunning it is to be alive, to be human for a short while . . . to touch skin, to touch life . . . to be able to hold one another.

> Even more striking was my growing realization that the nature of this human experience was up to me. Would I be driven by anger? Stubbornness? Fear? Protection? Love? CHOOSE THE ONE YOU WANT, as Morrie would say. He was busy choosing the way he wanted to die.

He looked down at his own hands, no longer able to do his bidding, and he let go with great thanks.

We shifted to hearing. The song of a bird. The resonance of the human voice. The familiar intonation of someone you love. Music. Morrie played Puccini at full volume, and wept for the beauty of sound and the fleetingness of the experience. He played *Madame Butterfly*, Maria Callas, Vivaldi's *Four Seasons*. And he wept, knowing that the brief lifetime during which we are able to listen to such sweetness is hardly long enough. He listened and remembered until he could say, "I'm grateful to have *ever* heard. The gift was profound. Now I let it go with gratitude."

Vision. The hibiscus plant in Morrie's study. Once he'd ignored it, now it was more than beautiful to him. Nature hadn't held much interest for him when he was walking about, but now that his field of vision was limited to what he could see from his window and what could be brought inside, sight acquired new meaning. He wondered whether he'd see another snowfall. He looked at human faces with renewed focus.

By the time we explored the sense of taste, Morrie could no longer swallow easily. He was now drinking only liquids, just as Helen had done when I'd visited her in Texas. But in terms of *our* process, Morrie became very creative. Unable to do his own tasting, he instructed me to go out and find tiramisu and eat it *for* him. We laughed about the number of things a person tastes during a lifetime. For Morrie, there were many tastes that he'd loved. Duck well prepared, potato latke . . . we laughed until we both cried because they seemed so incongruous when listed together. And then, grateful for the gift, he let it go. We moved to the sense of smell, and Morrie talked about the scent of a pale yellow rose, the fragrance of rhododendrons. And lest it all sound too sublime and soulful, it was all, always, interspersed with Morrie's devilish nature and sharp wit, with his humor and irreverence. In the thick of the most poignant remembrances, I arrived one Friday to be greeted by a string of directives from Morrie. *Please shut the door right now. Move this. Fix that. Sit down.*

I finally had had enough. "Morrie, you're still telling me what to do," I complained.

The right eyebrow arched and the eyes danced. He cocked his head. "And you're still doing it," he declared emphatically. Vintage Morrie.

When the remembrances had all been spoken, we decided to give one another a last gift, something to commemorate this journey. I gave Morrie the small string of love beads I'd made with Scott during the extraordinary year we'd spent walking together. Then I told him about Scott. His eyes misted. The beads had moved from the hands of a young boy to those of an old man. I had my own feelings. I'd been lucky enough to walk with both of them.

Morrie's gift to me was from his bookshelf. A worn and treasured copy of Martin Buber's I AND THOU, a book whose pages encompass the relationship that exists between a human being and the transcendent God.

Throughout these months I had been working on the manuscript for my fourth book, which would become *Gift of the Red Bird*. In the book I describe the vision quest I made in the desert in south central Texas. Morrie kept telling me to hurry. He so wanted to read this story, and he was afraid he wouldn't live past the date of publication. Characteristically, he pushed me to bring the manuscript to his house and read it to him ahead of time, just in case. We set aside one particular afternoon, and I did read Morrie the unedited pages.

In the story, a red cardinal guides and befriends me as I confront both myself and my fears in the wilderness. In uncanny and powerful ways, the bird continues to show up throughout my three days and nights and becomes for me an unquestioned sign of God's presence and protection. When I finished reading, Morrie voiced his skepticism. His reaction surprised me since he'd been in tears when I read about the bird's uncanny appearance following a stormy night. Ever the scientist, ever questioning, he finally asked, "Do you truly believe that such things have meaning? That the occurrences are not by total coincidence?"

It was a lovely moment. I turned to the window, and Morrie followed my gaze. Only then did he see what I had been watching for the last ten minutes. A red cardinal was sitting at his windowsill, looking in at us. It had arrived as I read about its appearance in the story. Even Morrie was impressed.

"Don't push the river," says my friend Richard Rohr. Don't get ahead of your soul. The goal isn't to get somewhere. The goal isn't about forcing something to happen. The goal is to be in harmony with the gifts that are already given. The goal is to fall into your life.

I watched Morrie fall into his life. I watched him move from the resolution made by a defiant nine-year-old boy angry at God for taking his mother . . . through the scientist's certainty that "the need to find God is only a desperate attempt to preserve the ego" . . . to the old man who proclaimed that "nothing really matters but love."

Bit by bit Morrie let go of the things that didn't matter, and learned that his dignity came from his inner self.

When Ted Koppel interviewed Morrie for a third and final session on *Nightline*, Morrie summed up his philosophy with these words: *Compassion, love, responsibility, and awareness. And we all learn it too late. If we could only see things the way they are, rather than the way we want them to be*. It reminded me of the words of author Stephen Levine, "We bury the very things that might set us free."

The greatest letting go, of course, is the ultimate letting go of life. "How would you approach it?" Morrie wanted to know.

I didn't know. "It's not something you can simulate," I told him. "You can't imagine the imminence of death when you're still convinced that you have time." But characteristically, Morrie pressed.

"Well," I ventured, "I think I'd imagine a pair of outstretched arms, into which I'd fall when I was ready."

"You believe a person can determine when they're ready to go?"

"Maybe. Many have done so. If you're no longer holding on, and are willing to let go, what would stop you?"

Morrie was thoughtful. Then alert. "Whose arms would those be?"

It made me laugh. Clearly, he would debate theology to the end. But that was Morrie. It was the uniqueness of his spirit. "Morrie," I said, choosing my words with care, "the name by which your mind knows those arms isn't the point. Your spirit knows. Frankly, I think the name is secondary. It's the falling into them that is so difficult."

"Well," he wanted to know, "if those arms *were* a name I didn't speak, and couldn't recognize, would they still catch me?"

I drew a deep breath and decided to give a simple, one-word answer. "Yes. That's what I believe. Yes."

Morrie could never leave it there. "Why?"

"Because in the act of falling back, your heart would be fully open and trusting . . . finally abandoned to Spirit."

In the weeks that followed, Morrie asked me dozens of times to tell him the story of falling back into the outstretched arms. He always closed his eyes when I talked.

"Just picture going to sleep," I would say. "You've let go of everything. There's nothing left to stop you. Let go and you'll be caught."

I visited Morrie for the last time on a Thursday evening in November. His family had called to say that he was weakening. He was in a hospital bed by now, and one eye opened slowly when I came into the room. He smiled weakly as I took his hand. "Tell the story," he mouthed. His words were barely intelligible, but I knew what he was asking because he had asked so often. I told him the story and then sat with him as he slept. When the attendant returned to check on him, I looked back one last time and left. Ultimately that sleep continued, deepening into the coma that carried Morrie away. He died on Saturday morning, serenely and peacefully, just as he had hoped to do.

His funeral was held at Brandeis University, where he'd taught with such enthusiasm and life. Hundreds of young men and women were guided by his knowledge, and they came at the end to pay their respects. I was in Connecticut when Morrie's wife called to tell me he had died, so I had a two-hour car ride in which to sort through my own feelings.

Morrie had challenged me. He pushed me to break the rules, and he gave me the opportunity to look through his eyes, WITH HIM, at his approaching death.

My last emotion was gratitude.

Morrie and I had an important conversation when his life first began to change dramatically, thrusting him into the public eye. He had just taped the first of three interviews with Ted Koppel for *Nightline*, and the response had been overwhelming. Because of *Nightline*, Mitch Albom reappeared in Morrie's life and was beginning to meet with him on Tuesdays to write a book about Morrie's death and dying. As all of this was unfolding, Morrie sat me down. He'd done a lot of thinking, and he wanted me to be honest with him.

Would I be hurt, he wanted to know, if his public interviews and his book with Mitch didn't mention the journey he and I were taking together? Our therapeutic sessions, of course, would never be revealed. That was not at issue. But the Friday journey was separate. In fact he *wanted* me to share that journey, once he died, hoping our experiences might offer solace or perhaps guidance for others. But while his life was still being lived out, it was something he wanted to keep private. His life was already turned inside out . . . so much of it given away. *"If I give this too,"* he reasoned, *"I'm not sure it will have the same integrity. I need to have something that still belongs only to me. Something I'm living, but not revealing."* I understood, and I agreed. It was similar to writing entries in your diary thinking that one day those thoughts would be published. The honesty of the writing would be immediately compromised.

From time to time over the past decade, and mostly in retreat settings, I have spoken about my "human being" conversations with Morrie. There has always been a strong response.

Morrie was walking a road we will all walk, and the choices he faced are common to everyone. We all decide the extent to which we'll open our hearts.

We decide whether or not life is an incomparable gift. We decide how gracefully and fully we'll respond to disappointment and loss, or whether we'll finally yield to the things that cannot be changed. Morrie stood at an inner threshold and decided to cross, reaching for a deeper love. As I finally put this story into words, allowing it to find its way to larger places, I'm aware that I'm doing exactly what I watched Morrie do. I'm letting go, this time for both of us.

Life, Tea, and Death at My Father's Table

BECAUSE MORRIE WAS URGING ME TO DO SO, I began visiting my father on a regular basis. His voice was always in my ear. *Resolve things. Get it right now, before it's too late.* One particular evening was especially poignant. My father was having surgery the next morning, and I had come to spend the night and drive him to the hospital early the next morning. In the middle of the night I heard him walking around. He couldn't sleep. I crept downstairs and stood in the doorway between the living room and the kitchen. My father was standing next to the kitchen table, the fingers of his right hand spread on the edge of its smooth surface. He didn't hear me, so I stayed in the shadows and watched. He was a short man, bald, with a distinctive hook in his nose, the result of a break that had never been set. His hands were small and thick, but even so, he played piano easily and well, with the lightest touch. When he played he stared into the distance, his eyes dark and unfathomable.

He was deep in thought when I entered the room that night, and I wondered what he was thinking. He walked to the large window at the head of the table and looked out at the moon. I asked myself whether he'd be alive in twenty-four hours to see the moon again. Was he asking the same thing? Then he moved slowly toward the living room, and I stepped back into the shadows. He stopped in front of the large, white recessed bookshelves that filled the right-hand wall and picked up the framed pictures of his children and grandchildren that were displayed there. He held them, one by one.

The moment was sad and discomforting. I was already deep in the throes of life and death with Morrie. Now I was watching my own father face his mortality. But it was easier with Morrie because there was no history. In this house there was not only history, but a difficult one. There were resentments and misunderstandings. For whatever reason, my father had found it very difficult to express approval and love, and our family lived with the tension of the strong emotions that warred inside him. But since we could never name them, or see them, we remained impotent against an invisible world he kept secreted deep within.

And there I was, in the middle of the night, wondering what I had always wondered. What was he feeling? And how could I bridge the distance between us? Was there some way to approach his hidden self? I finally made myself visible and asked him if he'd like to talk or have a cup of tea. He shook his head, no, but neither one of us moved. We were both facing the bookcase, looking in the same direction, standing side by side. I cautiously raised my hand and let it touch his shoulder. He still didn't move, so I began rubbing his back. Little, circular motions. Small patterns that contained a lifetime of longing, traced on his robe. He didn't respond, but he didn't pull away. At least he wasn't alone, and maybe that mattered.

We drove to the hospital early the next morning, and my father was prepped for surgery. When my mother and I rejoined him, he lay shivering on a gurney, waiting to be wheeled into the operating room. His prostate was enlarged, and there were malignant tumors in his bladder. He looked so disempowered in this setting. Was this the tyrant? The man whose moods commanded the household . . . the stern authority who listened to no one? I stood beside him, my insides churning. I couldn't bear his vulnerability, his nakedness.

I found a nurse and told her that my father was cold. She immediately brought a heated blanket and placed it over his thin hospital gown. I tucked the blanket around his feet and moved back to his side. He smiled his thanks and reached up to squeeze my hand, and there was perhaps more intimacy in that gesture than had ever passed between us. Even when the anesthesiologist appeared to give the shot that would put him out, he didn't let go. Finally his eyes closed, but I didn't step aside until they asked me to leave. I leaned over and whispered *Don't be afraid*, but the drug had already taken effect. As soon as the gurney was out of sight, I raced for the restroom and heaved out my insides. It felt as if I were heaving out all the pain my heart had ever held.

My father survived his surgery, and as he recovered I made an important determination. My focus (my selfish focus) had always centered on my disappointment that our relationship was so limited. That we couldn't speak to one another. That I never knew if he was pleased or displeased. I felt cheated. He was not a demonstrative man. He was not the kind of father I needed. Over the years I gave great power to my complaints, and I allowed my disappointment to justify extended periods when I wouldn't visit or call. I simply stayed away.

Now it occurred to me that my father may not have been an expressive, loving father . . . but I had not been a particularly loving daughter, either.

The pain went both ways. He got cheated too. I remembered visits when I had barely acknowledged him . . . or when I spoke with animation to my mother, but never looked toward him. Some of Morrie's words pushed at me: *If only we could see people the way they are, and not the way we want them to be.*

My father was a real person, and I had never seen that person. I measured whoever he truly was against the image in my mind. I laid out my conditions. He didn't even need to show up. No wonder he hadn't. I was wed to the father I wanted. And now, at this late date, what if I withdrew those conditions? Was it possible to relate to my father without imposing my own expectations? What if I began visiting him seeking *nothing* . . . only visiting because that's what I'd chosen to do . . . because that's the person, the daughter, I wanted to be. I was no longer a child. I needed to grow up and behave like the grown woman I was. I needed to love.

Realistically, I knew that visiting my father more regularly would bring mixed results. Sometimes it might feel good. At other times I assumed it would continue to be difficult. But I now saw that my father's behavior was irrelevant to this venture. His actions had to cease being a condition of *my* loving. My loving had to be in my own hands. It occurred to me with a real start: *Any love dependent on someone else's behavior wasn't love in the first place.* Did I want to *be* loved or did I want to love?

I began using the hour-long drive back to my parent's home to think about love, and to think about the person I wanted to be. One cost of loving without expectation was giving up blame. I was no longer a child dependent on someone else's care. What *had been* was past. Was I really willing to let my first, limited understanding of love be the final say, defining how I would love today? It was a choice. My father's purpose in life was not to match *my* inner image of a father. In fact, his purpose in life was no business of mine at all. I had my own purpose to tackle. I had to let a greater love begin to inform my heart.

After making weekly visits for two months, something shifted. I no longer rated my visits as good or bad. I stopped feeling happy or sad based on my father's mood. I went to see him because I wanted to. Sometimes he seemed appreciative, and sometimes not. It mattered less and less, until it didn't matter at all.

Having removed my own needs and expectations from the equation, all that remained was the person who was my father, and I began to see that person. I discovered a man for whom life had not been particularly happy and someone limited in making the connections with others that yield fullness and meaning. I saw his frailty, and the fear and insecurity that were his inner demons. And I wished, with all my heart, that his experience of life and work and family could have been so much more.

I'd spent over forty years feeling sorry for myself and holding grudges. The truth was that until now, even though we'd lived in the same house, I'd never seen my father at all.

In the final months of my father's life, just before his care demanded a nursing facility, we sat at the kitchen table whenever I came to visit.

The kitchen had always been the center of our home. Conversations began and ended around the table.

Made from a beautiful golden oak, the table originally had two leaves that were kept in the closet, ready to insert for company. On Sunday afternoons when I was growing up, the extended family would visit. Aunts, uncles, cousins. We gathered around the table with coffee and pastries, soda for the kids. When the children grew restless we'd run off to play, but the adults would sit and talk for long hours. The table was sturdy, with thickly grooved spindle legs that my father set on casters, to make it easier to move.

I vividly remember the day he decided to permanently glue the leaves into place and cover the oak top with Formica, which was the new technology. The act was utilitarian, without question . . . and over the years the Formica made quick work of spills. But the golden hued oak was art and beauty, and covering it up never settled well in my heart.

At that table we grew as a family, and mealtime was central. During those years whole families still gathered for dinner each evening. There were no conflicting sports schedules or after-school activities that ran late. Everything ended in time for families to come together. Even as a cheerleader, I don't remember missing dinner because of an evening game. I don't even remember rushing.

But the fact that we weren't rushing didn't mean our life was idyllic. We merely had longer "in house" hours in which to create havoc with one another. Great scenes took place at the table. My usual seat at the far end placed me opposite a large window. I loved sitting there because I could make faces at my reflection in the glass. My antics inevitably caused one of my sisters to laugh so hard she would be sent from the table. That never made sense to me. I was the instigator, and my parents sent *her* away, not me.

They never even changed my seat. But why would I point out that error?

At that table my father reviewed our report cards, helped us with math formulas, and delivered many a stern lecture. He was Italian, and even his conversational tone could feel like he was yelling. When he was displeased and being emphatic, the perception was doubly true. I was always scanning his face for signs of approval.

At that table my mother quizzed us on the questions in our Baltimore catechisms. Who made the world? *God made the world.* Why did God make us? *To know, love, and serve him in this world, and be happy with him forever in the next.* My mother wasn't even Catholic; she was Baptist. But she remained faithful to her promise that we'd be raised in the Catholic faith.

We sat at that table with friends, or when our dates were nervously being scrutinized by my father. We sipped tea there, late at night, if our stomachs were upset or we simply couldn't sleep. I sat at that table with Roy D'Arcy when he asked my parents for my hand in marriage. A year later we sat there together, presenting my parents with their first grandchild, Sarah. We bathed Sarah in a large, blue aluminum tub that we set on the table's broad surface.

I returned to that same table three years later, trying to make sense of Roy's and Sarah's deaths. And once my second daughter, Beth, was born (I was pregnant with Beth at the time of the accident), that's where I brought her. She too was bathed in the familiar blue tub. She too felt the familiarity and safety we'd all known in that space.

My father has now died, but my mother still lives in our original family home and the table is there, silent witness, still, to our meals, our conversations, our sadness, and our joy. But it has become a symbol to me of so much more. It represents the very traditions with which I was raised, and it serves as a reminder that in spite of the struggles we experienced in that home, Love was present. In the midst of discord and confusion, Love was at work. Neither our disappointments nor our limited grasp of Love were ever intended to be as far as we would advance.

The life lived at that table was meant to be our starting point. But we had to grow beyond it.

All along the way, ablaze in mystery and paradox, a larger Love waits to set us free. That was the Love that helped me recognize the restricting power of my expectations, and set me in the direction of real change. In a sense it heaved the Formica off my childhood table. The Formica had served a utilitarian purpose for a time. But ultimately, the leaves had to be unglued again, and the golden oak was exposed.

Love insists that everything be set free.

One night I dreamed that I walked into my childhood kitchen. My siblings, my mother, my daughter, Beth, were all there. But the table was gone. Vanished. We stood in the space where it had been, and the space had power. In the dream I understood that the former things had been intentionally cleared away. They had to be. All the old ways of perceiving and knowing were going to be replaced. In the great space where the table had once been was room for Spirit to move.

Everything
Lies
Before Us

SCOTT, THE YOUNG BOY WITH WHOM I WALKED when I was a therapist in training, is now middle-aged, with children of his own. I am still stunned by the way we came full circle, encountering one another during two seasons of our lives, both times with such significance. In granting permission for this story to be told, Scott wrote: "All the memories are positive and endearing. Thanks for caring so much and for walking with me."

John Bentley, to whom I gave the baby shoe pin, has remained in my life. John and his wife, Judy, eventually met my daughter, Beth, and Beth immediately loved them as I do. Our mutual friend, Marcia, repeated the story of the shoe and the Scripture verse to friends one day, and a woman who was listening timidly said, "I was the person who gave Paula the shoe." She explained that she often kept small items in her purse to give away, and on that particular day the baby shoes were all she had. Even though she felt strongly encouraged to offer them to me, she struggled against her impulse. It seemed cruel to give two little shoes to a mother who had two daughters, one of whom had died. But she decided to trust what was guiding her and reached her hand through the crowd that day.

Within a year following this experience, I stayed with John and Judy while passing through Alabama. They awakened me in the morning and told me that they intended to pay fully for Beth's college education. Their hearts had been impressed to do so. John said, "You will never see another tuition bill." And I didn't. They were taking seriously the Scripture admonishing believers to take care of the fatherless and the widows.

> They also explained that they needed to learn to give,
> not from their surplus, but at a cost.

In time, John sat down and told Beth the story of the baby shoe and gave it to her. So the shoe is now passed on. He assumed a fatherly role that day, and he sent her out to explore the far corners of the world.

Julia, the young woman I met in prison, has now been released. Three days after Thanksgiving, in November 2003, I stood at the Newton Center train station in Massachusetts, waiting for the train from Boston to arrive. The train pulled into the station at precisely 12:30 p.m., and Julia stepped off. A moment we'd imagined and dreamed about for many years was happening. Her sentence had been served. Julia was free.

It seems natural that we might have shed tears, but in fact, we laughed. We hugged one another and whirled around in a circle and laughed and laughed. No guards. No metal detectors. No restrictions. We found a small Indian restaurant and talked nonstop. We talked about the ceramic piece I had smuggled into the prison retreat years ago. We talked about some of the inmates I'd come to know. We talked about the remarkable fact that she was about to enter the School of Divinity at Boston University. There was not enough time to say all the words and express all the feelings.

After our meeting in Boston, Julia emailed to say that she'd spoken with her lawyer and learned that she will be denied a driver's license for the rest of her life. She *could* appeal and insist on a hearing, but the lawyer told her that the fight would be financially prohibitive, and she'd lose in the end anyway. She was philosophical in her email. "They want my license more than I do, so I think they should have it," she wrote. "Solzhenitsyn has a great saying: *You can have power over people as long as you don't take everything away from them. But when you've robbed a man of everything, he's no longer in your power.* Well, I'm saving myself the step of getting robbed—I'm passing go and collecting more freedom. And in a few minutes I'll be on my way to work—*walking* along the river."

I vividly remember the first night I visited Julia's prison. I thought I would be helping others. I told myself that I was bringing something of value to those less fortunate. I was so ill informed.

> The truth is that I had no idea how much I needed to be there, and how much would be given to me. The experience inside the prison was a mirror in whose glass I saw the reflection of many things.

There have been a number of prisons and shelters since then. Men and women of remarkable honesty have given me a glimpse of their courage. Every story reminds me of how little I know about freedom, and how the greater Love differs from the love we pursue.

My house in Texas remained unsold for seven months. Then one Thursday afternoon in September, I arrived for my weekly acupuncture appointment. The office was empty so I took a seat in the waiting room, stopping to select a magazine from the rack. I had seen Dr. Ho regularly for almost five years, and had come to love his quiet words and the quality of his caring. He was slim, with jet black hair and a bright, easygoing nature. He smiled easily and often. Of Vietnamese origin, he had lived in many countries and was deeply philosophical and thoughtful. When I was a fairly new patient, I learned that he both knew and had studied alongside the renowned Buddhist monk, Thich Nhat Hahn. Delighted that I was familiar with his mentor's work, especially his writings about love and peace, we had many lengthy conversations. Twice he gave me books to read, and he even came to one of my own book signings, which was unusually kind and supportive.

On this day he walked silently into the waiting room and sat down in a chair across from me. He smiled. *Did you sell your house yet?*

It was a question I'd been responding to for months. Everywhere I went the reminder was there. I shook my head. *No.*

Well, he said, I think I might buy it.

The words seemed so strange, coming from him, but perhaps would have struck me as equally incongruous coming that unexpectedly from anyone. It was the way he said it, with such ease, using the same intonation he might use to say, *Your treatment room is ready.* I laughed. "Yeah," I mumbled.

Then my treatment room *was* ready, and still shaking my head about our curious conversation, I prepared for my treatment. After the session, as I was writing out my check, Dr. Ho asked, "Would it be convenient for me to see your house at 5:30 today, when I'm on my way home?" (He lived an hour away, in San Antonio, and met with clients at this particular location only two days a week.) I was again startled. How far did he intend to carry this? I didn't take him seriously at all. But feeling awkward and unsure of how else to respond, I decided to be polite and said, "Well, yes."

He arrived as promised, and for over an hour I showed him my house and property. As we walked through the rooms and out into the yard, our conversation was a mixture of water systems, square footage, and theology. In the annals of real estate and house showings, I'm certain we skewed the curve. Finally Dr. Ho moved back inside and toward the kitchen counter. As he reached the bar stool in front of the counter, he turned and said, *Well . . . .*

I had anticipated this. *Well, thank you so much, but I don't think so.* These were the words I imagined. Or, *Well, I'm grateful for your time, but . . .*

He said neither. He pulled out the stool and sat down. *Well,* he finally continued, *I do in fact want to buy your house.*

The words were the words I had been primed to hear for over seven months. Words I *longed* to hear. But under these circumstances, they made little impression on me. I reminded myself to be sensible.

Your acupuncturist does not whimsically decide to buy your house. This cannot happen after someone casually walks through once, on a Thursday evening after work. Real estate is a ritual that moves in an entirely different way. I didn't know much, but I did know that.

Tell me, he said, oblivious to what I knew about real estate, *what amount of money do you need in order to make this move to the West Coast happen?* I stared blankly. How far was this conversation going to go? I was hungry and ready to cook dinner. When I didn't speak, he persisted. *In order to realize this dream, how much money do you need from this house sale?*

I found my voice. *It's not the way it's done,* I responded. *My asking price is based on the housing market. First you contact my realtor, and she'll give you all the details. Then you and she negotiate, she speaks with me and I respond, and then . . .*

His calm expression never changed. YOU'RE NOT LISTENING TO ME, he said. WHAT AMOUNT OF MONEY DO YOU NEED IN ORDER TO MOVE . . . IN ORDER TO CREATE THIS NEW START?

137

I swallowed hard and told him what I needed in order to move and begin this new adventure. He nodded his head, *Well, then that's what I'm offering.*

Without digesting the full power of his words, I immediately began arguing for us to return to the "rules." *You can't mean this,* I said, providing him with his return to sanity. *Your wife hasn't even seen the house.*

Oh, yes. That, he said. *We'll come by on Saturday, if you'll be home.*

I tried to decide whether I'd ever met anyone so determined. He left a few minutes later, apparently committed to buying my house. I watched his truck pull out of the driveway and thought, *No one lives like this.*

Saturday's visit with the Hos was essentially a repeat of Thursday's tour. He arrived with his wife, Michelle, who was beautiful and vivacious, with blond hair and a twinkle in her eye. Her sense of humor was infectious, and I liked her immediately. We walked through the rooms, stood on the decks, walked through the yard, mixing and matching questions about sewer systems with thoughts about the purpose and meaning of life. I was convinced that I'd now spent a total of three hours showing a house for reasons I might never understand. I thoroughly enjoyed the time we spent, but reason told me that the Hos could not be viable buyers. It had happened too quickly, too unconventionally. Completely forgotten in that moment was the fact that my decision to move and my willingness to leave were all about pushing past established ways of being. I can be sublimely blind.

The Hos stood firm. They were moving ahead with the craziness. Michelle finally said, *Paula, we'll give this our best shot.* She smiled. *This will be our third property.*

I tried to digest that fact. I knew that Dr. Ho had an office in San Antonio. But if they sold their San Antonio home and moved into mine, they would have only two properties, not three. Then the unthinkable occurred to me. Three properties? My mind was processing in slow motion, but I finally managed to say, "Aren't you planning to move into this house?"

No. At least, not right away. They stood there smiling in the fiery mid-afternoon sun. No? My mind raced, but I spoke very slowly, *If you aren't planning to move here, then why are you doing this?* I hesitated. *You're buying a house you don't need?*

They nodded. *It's my philosophy,* Dr. Ho finally replied. He smiled. *We support one another in life. That's the main point, isn't it?* I didn't move or breathe. He continued, *I've watched you waiting to take a new step. So I thought, maybe I can help make this happen. We are, after all, here for one another.* He looked around. *We feel the peace and harmony of this space. We'll take good care of this home.*

After the Hos left I climbed the stairs to my front deck and moved back inside the house. I wanted to call Roy, but I didn't know what to say. I paced, looking out the wall of windows at the beautiful Texas sky. Who lives this way, I kept asking myself? Who takes commitment and caring that seriously? Who goes into debt to that degree because "we're here for one another?" It was a level of love, a raw, unadorned love so stunning that its force brought tears. I had thought my own decision was bold. Hardly. All I had done was express an intention. But what I was looking at was not only bold, but beautiful. It was the actual living out of the freedom I wanted to embrace.

> Kindness. That was the word that came to me. But it
> was the quality of the kindness. Pure kindness. A force.
> And with that force, a glimpse of how we might live.

What's possible became actual that day through the gesture of two very tender people.

That night I remembered a poem by Naomi Nye entitled "KINDNESS." I dug it out of an old file and read these words:

Before you know kindness as the deepest thing inside,

You must know sorrow as the other deepest thing.

You must wake up with sorrow.

You must speak to it till your voice

catches the thread of all sorrows

and you see the size of the cloth . . .

Surely, at one time in my life, the "size of the cloth" had become known to me through sorrow. Burying a husband and young daughter in the same week had clothed me in that knowledge. But now, through a sheer experience of kindness, the opposite side of the cloth was glimmering before my eyes, a cloth almost too delicate to touch. I kept repeating to myself, *this is how we might live.* If our hearts were unbound, if we really fell into love and learned its secrets, *this is what might be possible.*

Am I ready? What would it mean to make a fresh start? To begin loving beyond the limits?

The Hos bought my home as an act of stunning kindness, and their "uncommon" love now sends me out to answer with my own life the question, *What would it mean to make a fresh start, together?* The magnificent nature of their act is still difficult to fully grasp. They had me keep a key to my Texas home, and they encouraged me to leave a bed and lamp so when I return to visit friends, I'll have a place to stay. They remind me that this journey is not done without community. We find our way together. They plan to take me to dinner the night before I board the plane for California.

In the still of the night I pay attention to the invisible part of me that first whispered *Go* when Roy asked me to set out from my comfortable life in Texas. There is a deepening sense that the place where I stand is the threshold my heart has always sought. I didn't know how to get myself here, but something within me did. That's how it happens.

Along the way I've learned that we avoid our own healing at great cost. Until the work of forgiveness is begun, until we learn the language of gratitude, until we understand the small nature of much that we call love, we will repeat the same patterns and miss the portals that might set us free.

The old dynamics are too compelling, the familiar ideas and beliefs too ingrained.

Thresholds demand a willingness to walk in new directions. They ask us to "not know"—we who are so in love with knowing. They insist that we be led where we never intended to go. They will not respect the hunger that feeds the ego and keeps us small. They speak of a Love far different from the one we know.

Some say there's a kind of detachment to the truest Love. That this is its nature. And that when the full power of Love is unleashed, even the stars are affected.

As I release this manuscript to be published, I do so from my new life in California. I have been here for only four months . . . too brief a time to have answers, or even direction. But long enough to know that I love the land, love the proximity to the bay, the hiking trails, the new friends I am beginning to embrace. Long enough to know that this was the right decision. I feel that rightness in the peace that blankets me from within. And I see it as I watch the way my friendship with Roy causes both of our lives to become larger. Everything expands as we move, together, toward the deeper experience of God that beckoned us all along. No one moves in or out of our circle without it seeming to us to be important. We pay attention differently. We relate to very mundane things from a different space.

When Harry Potter is trying to find the platform for the train that will bring him to his new school, he faces a blank wall where Platform 9¾ should be. Then the mother of a student who has made this trip before gives him advice. She encourages him to run right toward the platform (*the threshold*), promising that it will yield when he gets to it. That's what I'm learning: to trust the amount of light I *have* been given and run right toward the next doorway. I no longer want to take my cues from people who are themselves frightened. I don't want to spend my hours defending the last place from which I looked. I want to move toward this force that is forever pushing through the events in our lives. And that I should have a companion for this next leg of the journey feels very simple and very true. Everything lies before us.

Into the Mystery

Walking out,

stepping into nowhere,

falling from the inside

out,

there is a place

where you let go of everything

you thought your life

was about.

The walls are gone,

the comfort and the pushing

against them

fallen away,

and in the nothingness

of the mystery

you are held,

more real

than you were

yesterday.

— VICKY EDMONDS

Acknowledgments

The entire team at Crossroad Publishing has been an integral part of this book. In ways large and small they have each contributed to this manuscript's emergence, and I am immensely grateful for the growing we've done together. My appreciation to Maria Devitt, Jackie Andre, Matthew Laughlin, Christine Phillips, Jim Phillips, and especially John Jones. Although John is not my assigned editor, he is an incredible support, and always right there, at a moments notice, to talk through ideas, or share his unswerving belief in things. Just to think of him makes me glad. I greatly thank Gwendolin Herder, who is both my publisher and friend. Her openness, honesty, and willingness to listen have helped me turn significant corners as a writer.

Most of all I am grateful to my editor Roy M. Carlisle. In addition to being a dear and important friend, Roy is a gifted editor who continually opens up new vistas and says to me, "You can do this. Go for it." He has affected how I look at many things, what I think is possible, how I view myself as a writer, and what I am willing to risk. His love of books and his commitment to authors is notable. His commitment to our new adventure in California is a gift that grows each day, defying even my most generous words.

Thanks to my mother, who died so suddenly as this book was about to be printed, to my late father, to Scott, to Julia, to Morrie, to John and Judy Bentley, to Marcia Hodges, Pat Simmons, and to Michelle and Hoang Ho for the strong and wonderful stories that changed all our lives. They remind me that *this is it*, that no moment should be wasted, that the short journey we call a lifetime is filled with power.

I thank Robin and Jamshid Galehzan for their companionship ever since I arrived in California. In particular, I thank Robin for listening to the story of this book as it unfolded, adding her keen insights, and patiently and lovingly helping me get my bearings. I thank Jamshid for teaching me about the beauty of the poetry which threads its way through his culture in Iran, and for being an exceptional model of the power of a quiet and loving presence.

Grateful appreciation to Tony and Pam Petrotta, Jack Mingo and Erin Barrett, McNair Wilson, and Daphne Drescher for also opening their arms to a newcomer in their midst. Each of them made me feel immediately welcome in California by filling my life with good food, music, and laughter, as well as runs on the beach and around the lake.

Thanks to Madeline Tyng for once again taking photographs for me, and for the extraordinary way she allows me to share in her own recent loss of her husband, Tom.

Her beauty and strength, even in grief, convinces me that we *are* capable of so much more in our relationships.

Special appreciation to my dear friends Kaye Bernard, Denise Casey, Lisa Levy, Tom and Debbie Morrill, Connie Barrios and Stacey Dille for all the things they so willingly do to help me further both my speaking and the ministry of my Foundation.

And deepest thanks, always, to my daughter Beth, who is such a bright light in my world.

About the Author

Paula D'Arcy, a writer, retreat leader, and conference and seminar speaker, travels widely in the United States, Canada, and abroad. She is also President of the Red Bird Foundation, which supports the growth and spiritual development of those in need and furthers a ministry both to those in prison and those living in third world or disadvantaged cultures.

A former psychotherapist who has ministered to those facing issues of grief and loss, Paula worked with the Peale Foundation, founded by Dr. Norman Vincent Peale, from 1980 until his death in 1993. In recent years she has frequently teamed with Fr Richard Rohr in presenting seminars on the Male/Female Journey. Her individual work includes leading women in Initiation and Rites of Passage.

Paula's ministry grew from personal tragedy. In 1975 she survived a drunk driving accident which took the lives of her husband and twenty-one-month-old daughter. Pregnant at the time, Paula survived the accident to give birth to a second daughter, Beth Starr.

Paula lives in northern California

A Word from the Editor

The Crossroad Publishing Company seeks to contribute to the richness of life with fine books as a leader in spiritual, religious, and cultural publishing. We value the people with whom we work, our colleagues and our authors, all of whom we welcome as partners in our common venture.

In the more than twenty five years that I have been a part of this "common venture" the ground of publishing has shifted dramatically. And in many ways Paula D'Arcy is an exemplar of that shift. Allow me to explain. For many years writers and publishers were confined to the narrow straits of the denomination to which they belonged. So a book by a Methodist or Baptist or Presbyterian or Episcopalian or Roman Catholic clergy or layperson was published by that particular denominational publishing house. And it was read by laity or clergy in that particular denomination. This was generally true for every denomination, Protestant or Catholic, large or small, including the lesser known stepsisters such as evangelicals and pentecostals.

In the sixties and seventies a major shift began. The mainline denominations were losing members; all kinds of other movements were growing *across* denominational lines. Clergy and laity were shifting their allegiance from dying denominations to vital movements.[1] In other words the mode or particular way in which each person worked out their salvation and spirituality became primary. If their spiritual path was dominated by social action or contemplation or Biblical study or charismatic experiences or liturgical practices then those people "felt" closer to others who were so inclined, even if they were in other denominations. Although invisible, these lines of allegiance were not only profound but would change the religious landscape in this country forever. Religious publishing—magazine publishers figured this out before book publishers did—had a harder time following this shift but they tried.

Enter writers like Paula D'Arcy who had the ability to cross denominational lines because of their particular emphasis. One of my own mentors, Richard J. Foster, has outlined his paradigm for these emphases in spiritual life as follows: the contemplative tradition, the holiness tradition, the charismatic tradition, the social justice tradition, the evangelical tradition, and the incarnational tradition.[2] What publishers discovered was that there were writers who were the preeminent voices in each of these fields. And those writers became the most

[1] The core of this set of ideas emerged for me in a conversation with Jim Wallis in the early 90s. As a magazine publisher he was attuned to these issues.

[2] Foster, Richard J., Streams of Living Water: Celebrating the Great Traditions of Christian Faith (HarperSanFrancisco, 1998).

sought after and the best selling authors for publishers. For example when a reader is looking for a book in the social justice field the names of Joan Chittester or Jim Wallis emerge over and over, or for the incarnational tradition the names Henri Nouwen or Joyce Rupp or Fredericka Matthews Green are unavoidable, or in the evangelical tradition the names of Hannah Whitehall Smith or PhilipYancey or Billy Graham or Max Lucado might pop up. And in the contemplative tradition most readers will recognize the names of Evelyn Underhill or Barbara Brown Taylor or Thomas Merton or Thomas Keating or Paula D'Arcy. But what I would bet money on is that most readers could not name the denominational affiliation of each of these writers. The shift is complete.

For many of these writers, and here is where Paula D'Arcy is an exemplar, their style and message even goes beyond just crossing denominational lines to crossing religious lines and then even out into the broader world of people concerned about topics of human interest. Paula has accomplished that rare goal with this book.

Even more profound than that accomplishment is the rare but luminous authenticity that shines through this set of stories. All of us are hungry for this kind of writing and even more importantly for this kind of living. We want to know that Paula D'Arcy is a real person who actually lives the words she breathes out to us. I can tell you that she is that real person and that it gives me hope in all things spiritual, as it will you.

This book is a memoir, a slice of Paula's story that tells us about a particular issue. And it is in today's memoirs that most of us find and enjoy our stories of authentic spirituality. Several years ago a book agent friend told me that editors in New York were certain that the "memoir fad" was over and that she should not try to sell them any more memoirs. I laughed. People didn't want to read true personal stories any more? That was and is a ludicrous idea. And the "fad" is now as strong as ever and continues to be one of the staples of publishing. And this is especially true for those of us who live as close as we know how, to that thin "veil" between ordinary life and spiritual life. Paula takes us there and for a few moments we glimpse beyond the veil. You can trust her as your guide.

— Roy M. Carlisle
Senior Editor